ORCINUS ORCA
Song of the Ocean

N.B.J.Clayton

Other epic poems by this author:

Kibeho: An Epic Poem
Afghan: Song of the Desert
Hollandia Nova, 1712: Song of the Coast

WARNING!

Warning! Kulinma! Ngulakujaku-kula!

This book might contain names of people who have since departed this world.

Copyright © N.B.J.Clayton, 2020

N.B.J.Clayton asserts the moral right to be identified as the owner of this work.

All rights reserved. No part of this publication may be reproduced, stored in a retrieval system, or transmitted in any form, by any means: electronic, mechanical, photocopying, recording or otherwise, without the prior permission of the copyright owner of this book.

This book is sold subject to the conditions that it shall not be resold, hired out or otherwise circulated, except in its original binding.

Publication data:

Orcinus Orca: Song of the Ocean, 1st ed.
ISBN 978-0-6487672-6-8

HIS004000   HISTORY / Australia & New Zealand
NAT019000   NATURE / Animals / Mammals
POE014000   POETRY / Epic

SONG OF THE OCEAN

FOR GEOGRAPHY:

Google Maps is a fantastic way in which to find your way around [especially in satellite mode] Eden. Place names and general locations mentioned, with regards to Eden and Twofold Bay, are easily scrutinized. Distances are easily depicted, providing essential assistance and advantage, where a printed map within this book could never do nearly the same in scope or dimension, as may be appropriate to this story.

IMPORTANT NOTE:

Some of the evidence and general information concerning Typee and Jackson, during examination, appears misconstrued and does differ vastly: as to whether or not they are one and the same, I do not know, but I have favoured the opinion that they are two individuals.

This is a work of historical-fiction and should not be used as a source on which to base the history of our protagonists, for whaling events over time have been pruned and extended, rightly or wrongly, to bring to light the charismatic behaviour of the interaction between man and killer whale as best as possible; but it is better to apply the 'historical-fiction' tag than be cursed for telling an untruth that I may not have been sure about. In the chapter 'Mother of Mary' I have completely fabricated the events surrounding the interactions of Orcinus: who is it to know whether or not such attempts by killer whales was made, but it was the thing that was likely to occur if the opportunity did arise: consider

ORCINUS ORCA

it far-fetched or romantic, that is up to you, but where there are no survivors then there is no truth or lie. And last but not least, Orcinus orca is of the oceanic dolphin family: a dolphin.

FAST FISH

A harpoon entering the body of a whale did not kill it; it was meant only as a means by which to secure the line and maintain a measure of control over the whale whilst lancing took place and the animal then killed; this might take some time and some number of lances. It was therefore not surprising to see that a rule was employed by which means a crew could announce quite categorically that 'it' owned the right to the whale in which its harpoon was attached; it went something like this: where the harpoon shall remain in the fish so struck, and a line or boat shall be attached thereto and continue in the power of the striker or headsman, such whale shall be deemed a fast fish, and although struck by any secondary or subsequent harpoon shall be the property of the first striker or headsman only.

COMMON BOAT LAYOUT

Twenty-nine feet long and pointed at both ends with a sag in the middle, wider in breadth around where the centre thwart lay, each differing slightly but built objectively the same, depending on the maker. There was planking across the first 4.9 feet of the stern where the loggerhead could be found, a short post where line was checked, it being drenched with buckets of water during hectic times when whales took off with the line attached, the friction of which was quite easily capable of seeing the loggerhead burn. Tubs which contained the line (fed through the loggerhead) were found between the middle and aft thwarts, depending on the headsman, 200 fathoms of line (manila rope) to each. The line was fed through the loggerhead and continued on through a niche in the bow, under an iron bar and then back over it to the harpoon, where it was attached securely. A typical boat would have anywhere from 5-8 oarsman, the number most favoured being that which allowed for an equal number of oarsman to be positioned either side of the boat once the battle against a whale was commenced, a number derived upon by the headsman.

From the bow the following positions were normally filled: harpooner, bow-oarsman, midship-oarsman, tub-oarsman, after-oarsman, headsman (at the stern); each seated upon his own thwart. The headsman was responsible for exchanging places with the harpooner once delivery of weapon had been secured within the beast, the harpooner responsible for securing 'fast fish'. The headsman, once having exchanged places with the harpooner, would then deliver as many lances as was required to fulfil his duty. The harpooner now controlled the sweep (steering oar) with great precision, it being 22-27 feet in length.

ORCINUS ORCA

THE FAMILY TREE

Parent:	Offspring:	3rd Gen
Stranger [F]	Tom [M]	
	Hooky [M]	
Typee [M]		
Humpy [F]	Walker [M]	
Cooper [M]	Young Ben [M]	
Big Ben [F]	Albert [F]	Charlie Adgery [M]
Jackson [M]	Brierly [M]	
Sharkey [F]	Skinner [M]	
Jimmy [M]	Kinscher [F]	
Big Jack [F]	Little Jack [M]	

SONG OF THE OCEAN

PROLOGUE 1: GENERAL INFORMATION

Killer whales; the orca; they are black and white,
Dolphin killers, mammals of the ocean, vigorous, full of might,
Warm-blooded creatures at the top of the food chain,
Man of the land the occasional invader and its only stain.

Their upper and dorsal surface is black and dorsal does tower,
Ventral surface and the face, be known, and much lower,
White with a saddle patch upon their back,
Light coloured underbelly of which black it does lack.

All gels and blends with the surface,
As through the ocean they grace,
For being viewed from above they confuse,
To lose in game hide and seek they do refuse.

Orca attack from below, is confusion: the dark patches,
A head on attack like masquerading shadows, misfortune latches,
Attack from high prey confused: underbelly camouflage,
Ignorance is bliss for Orcinus and so says the adage.

Hence their colouring plays important role,
From the churning jaws so hungry they do not dole,
Blazing head, dark upper, light under, secures his hunt,
Salmon easy victim, as for any, conned, fooled, great stunt.

ORCINUS ORCA

Menacing and mighty jaws,
One of the many ocean laws,
Killers mouth a big deal,
Always able to secure a meal.

A dorsal fin stands 5.9 feet at best,
Like a gigantic sail upon surface, seemingly at rest,
Though female in much smaller in comparison,
Signature of the ocean, steer wide on sight for good reason.

All rekindles the melody of 'ebony and white',
Black patches of death and angel white delight,
They escape all lucidity,
This is their great security.

A distinctive pigmentation,
Is also of the mention,
Behind the dorsal as though written in text,
An identification mark, one member from the next.

Tail flukes have no skeletal support but are more fibrous,
Propulsion from powerful movement of the tail stock enormous,
Eyes are suited to both ocean and air, vital, do astound,
killers lifting head out of the water to spy on ocean and ground.

Sight plays a major role in the killer's day to day life,
Being as good above the waves as it is below, strategy most rife,
Sound an important ability, able to decipher and rate,
Food seemingly placed before them like dinner upon plate.

SONG OF THE OCEAN

Of all the mammals of the ocean they travel narrows and girth,
    Widely distributed across all waters of the earth,
Well versed with the oceans of the globe: one as good as the rest,
Although mid-ocean activity is considered less, miniscule at best.

    Why this? to preserve energy and feast on flesh,
    To feeding grounds well tour and inwardly mesh,
To appease its rituals and endeavours, some seemingly unclean,
Tossing seals, eat rump of a porpoise, feast on tongue of baleen.

    Traversing along latitudes of both hemisphere,
    When and where temperature most suitably appear,
    Close to coastlines where fertility is at its highest,
Leisurely creatures of measurable existence, the mightiest.

    With its mouth of teeth, purely owned, no prize,
    Born of torpedo-shaped body and of immense size,
It can outplay, out manoeuvre, chase down and intercept,
Extremely intelligent, brain 3 times larger than mans', not inept.

With ability to undertake daily choirs, having great resilience,
Feelings of loneliness and despair, able to hold a grievance,
Can decipher incoming sounds, piece together any required action,
Intelligent, communicative, as a species does travel by faction.

They can be classified into three main groups, to each a flavour,
Each depicting their general displays of feeding and behaviour,
A matriarchal society whereby there is a strong bond and law,
And a structured group be it 'resident', 'transient', or 'offshore'.

ORCINUS ORCA

'Resident'; no dispersal of individuals from the group does flare,
Dispersal does not occur, quite simply, extremely rare,
Very large groups, pods of related killers, of desire and wish,
Dozens upon dozens who feed exclusively on squid and fish.

A mother, her sons and daughters, 3-10 killers at her side,
Contribute to a group of several dozen per pod, of laws abide,
Matrilineal binding linking all within, agile and full of ability,
Several hundred animals evident in its sustained community.

Matrilineal groups within a pod are created with equal charge,
And where the size of any pod becomes stretched and is too large,
Command and structure form break-away groups of the same,
A sub-pod of matrilineal society is created, well cast, not lame.

Vocal strategies within a sub-pod are adherent and extensive,
Strategies to remain throughout their lives and conductive,
Repertoire of dialect given, to some degree, to another sub-pod,
Or drawn from another as though in agreeance and with nod.

Sub-pods are a 'constant' to which members respond,
Remaining steadfast for the life of the matriarch, possibly beyond,
A killer will not usually defect from one sub-pod to another,
Although extensions from a sub-pod can be created from larger.

Pods also shared their complex mannerisms and talent,
Of their social and vocal range as though valiant,
Including their specific and unique language, never to neglect,
Call it accent or basic understanding of a different dialect.

SONG OF THE OCEAN

The 'transient' are less social than our former, the 'resident',
Travel in smaller groups of six or less, seemingly more violent,
Feed upon sea lions, seals and porpoises, given any chance,
Similarly cast may be a throng of thugs at a glance.

'Offshore' constitutes a large group, 30-60 the norm,
Preferring open waters to feed on fish, weathering any storm,
Predatory habits are harnessed, respectful to others highly noted,
An array and vast resources of food seemingly not exploited.

Food, we have touched upon, is as variable as the variety,
Feeding upon distinctive forms of prey for the majority,
The world a large plate upon which is found many a staple,
Penguin, seabirds, dugong, turtle, and manatee, as an example.

Humpbacks are also a heavenly source of food,
Orcinus devouring each, of which they are forever in the mood,
Australia is a known pantry of fat and tongue,
Easy to score, most easily won.

Humpbacks enjoy a frolic near Eden as they follow the coast,
Their migration route in range of Twofold Bay for the most,
From Antarctica, to the north, they travel in groups as we know,
Their migratory range and location the Orcinus in brain do stow.

Most of its life, under the waves, out of view, unique and large,
An orca will stalk its prey like the predator it is, never to barge,
To secure food the orca must act, with complete stealth,
Await the order to move in for the kill, nourishment is wealth.

ORCINUS ORCA

Large amounts of food it does need, without stretch of a lie,
And without substantial it will most surely die,
If food becomes bare bone, it can sustain self for many a week,
On little to no food, as its demise begins to speak and to peak.

Lack of food isn't the only killer,
Of the orca there is another miller,
For man also plays his hand in its demise,
Cruel and efficient whaling programmes for future to criticize.

Baleen whales, as example, are taken from their dinner plate,
Cleansed from the oceans, hence decreasing numbers to date,
Henceforth arrives the inability to feed as required,
A drop in the population of the killer seen as it is retired.

When food becomes scarce the killer will draw from within,
Energy taken from its high-calorie reserves of blubber under skin,
Its huge bulk serving as a means to survive,
Weeks without food can turn into months, now barely alive.

The Orcinus is able to hold back death for so, so many a day,
But age, whether young or old, decides this length of stay,
Age can alter the survival rate of a killer more readily,
One in mid-life stage of growth able to adapt more steadily.

And there is a strategy in its 'food for the picking',
Young seals or sea lions are preferred for the killing,
Adults rarely being attacked and for good reason, not stupidity,
Adults are dangerous, causing great injury, if given opportunity.

SONG OF THE OCEAN

The killers can purposely beach themselves upon the land,
Upon pebbled beach to take a seal pup in its teeth so grand,
Pups that consider the shoreline safe and clear of harm's way,
It is called 'stranding', just another means to secure its prey.

Killers have mastered this skill which is called 'stranding',
Females teach their young as though taking class with discipline,
Occasionally juveniles appear to do this in slow motion,
Not so much for play, but to harness the skill to perfection.

Juveniles may strand themselves by fault during this ride,
Adults coming to the rescue, stranding themselves alongside,
Aiding them back into the water most sublime, their biome,
Most sublime is their atmosphere, their biosphere, their home.

Or act as a decoy,
Thrashing in water as though to annoy,
Distracting pups so immature and unaware,
Orcinus acting with speed, with menacing glare.

It will shake its victim mercilessly and seemingly for thrill,
Though often simply and maliciously to disorientate and kill,
Killers will also take their prey to the pod, their clan,
To feed all equally, calves coming first, always part of the plan.

The calves might then play with their meal,
Harnessing techniques on the killing, life to steal,
Its prey, its captive, meeting its demise,
Lessons to learn as in all of life, no surprise.

ORCINUS ORCA

A seal might hide within small cave or rock crevice beneath,
A method to extract taken into hand causing much grief,
Two killers will take turns in surfacing and taking a breath,
One maintaining its watch upon the crevice to deliver death.

Once the seal runs out of air,
Tries to escape and in comes the pair,
Always there will be one killer, one at least,
To secure the meal, these orca are an intelligent beast.

They can hold their breath for 5 to 15 minutes in a dive,
216 fathoms or more, for great depth they strive,
Evolution has provided them with unique ability,
In the consumption of oxygen, a necessary commodity.

It is able to exchange gasses more readily,
Each breath manipulated with great ability,
With different ways to cater for different dives and situation,
Being shallow or deep, never a single choice, deny negation.

Its rib cage can collapse under insurmountable pressure,
Surplus air collecting beneath the blowhole in good measure,
And is able to store oxygen reserves in nasal passage,
In its bodily fluid and muscle tissue, their appendage.

Also store in red blood cells of body lean,
Their bodies are a mean machine,
Further more endowed,
Its heart beat can be slowed.

SONG OF THE OCEAN

Slow the heart for a deep dive with little strain,
Oxygenated blood diverted to heart and the brain,
Able to reabsorb blood nitrogen when comes the flood,
Avoiding the formation of killer bubbles in the blood.

When a calf enters its watery world, surfacing for the first time,
To satisfy its need to survive it gulps in air most sublime,
The mother and the calf's breathing then becomes synchronized,
Will remain so for much of their lives, to rigidly harmonize.

Their breathing aligned now a great benefit, she the instructor,
The mother becoming somewhat of a conductor,
And the remainder of the pod will take its breathing from her,
From this a great symphony, as though purposely she did stir.

For the needs of one and for all,
The remainder of the pod in her thrall,
For the maintenance of good health,
Food, food, food, their constant forage for wealth.

Generations of hunting tactics are taught to the young,
First-hand knowhow for abilities and success to them flung,
Crucial skills passed down from one generation to the next,
Skills individual and social, readily fed as though from text.

Calves acquire the ability to hunt on their own by month six,
Vocalizations and echolocation techniques thrown into the mix,
Social protocol and hunting strategies, good maintenance,
They mimic lessons from mothers all with great patience.

ORCINUS ORCA

They usually place great distance between pods,
Travel in the same direction, echolocation, the clearest of nods,
When they encounter food they will noisily leap and splash,
In the water and upon surface to lash and lash.

This does signify the find, often with vocalized message,
Though use of sonar is questionable: no clear sign of passage,
Due to alerting specific prey of their presence, may remain mum,
In particular dolphins and other mammals, 'never beat that drum'.

They devour creatures great and small,
Fish and whales, it matters not, for all their gall,
They know they are at top of the food chain and all is fair game,
A kill is a kill, to them it is all the same.

SONG OF THE OCEAN

PROLOGUE 2: FLESH OF FISH

A message is received from another pod, a neighbour,
A school of fish close by, the hunt more fun than labour,
Three pods move in to take position and further delve,
Force the school to surface, a single orca, of the hammer, a helve.

Together strong, the school compacted smaller and smaller,
Orcinus then vocalize each move, coordinated is each attacker,
Flash their white markings, a thunder, bad weather,
A school which does panic and then set upon by orca together.

The killers slap the water with their flukes performing magic,
Stunning the herring to stupidity, now seemingly static,
The killers taking a mouthful or two of their prey, these fish,
And take turns so that each has an equal share of the dish.

An orca beneath flashes again his white underbelly,
The herring continue in their panic, grouped tight in rally,
Remaining near the surface where they are in need,
No escape, now taken into mouth, flesh on which to feed.

A burst of fluke-bashing is then commanded by the matriarch,
Further stunning the herring, devoured, their death rather stark,
Taken into jaws as quickly as they float unconscious,
Other orcas continue to keep the herring massed, some oblivious.

ORCINUS ORCA

Easily corralled and now ready to feed upon flesh they are,
Another killer gets its fill and retreats but not far,
Orcinus orca taking turns to feed upon the herring,
Working as a team, coordinated, minds of strong bearing.

Once all have fed and had their fill,
The killers turn and depart, in for a meal, not the thrill,
Leaving the remaining herring to disperse,
Into deeper water for the school to nurse.

Some bodies half eaten or bitten do remain afloat,
Be they full or half devoured, their gases no time to bloat,
For they are picked up by birds of prey from the wave,
Swooping down to take what's left of the pickings from grave.

SONG OF THE OCEAN

PROLOGUE 3: FLESH OF WHALE

Some find larger morsels more rewarding,
A blue whale, being 59 feet in length, most appealing,
Soon surrounded by a deployed pod of experience,
Killers swim either side and below, currently no lenience.

Prevent the whale from making a move towards deep water,
They move in closer and at high speed to slaughter,
Allowing their presence to be known, to cause strife,
Maintaining the fear factor to penetrate as though a knife.

Those either side create white water, like snowy hail,
As they continue alongside the luscious blue whale,
Some move to the front, to slow down any attempt of escape,
Others behind prevent it turning, this bulk, this monstrous shape.

They disturb the whale's rhythm of breath,
They snap their mouths open and closed, predicting sweet death,
Gnashing their teeth together, to terrify their catch,
The chase continues for 20 miles, a lengthy battle, a match.

The blue whale feels self remorse, it does quickly tire,
The killers move in one at a time and then momentarily retire,
Take great hunks of flesh from the whale as he swims on,
The attack continues for five hours, the killers no longer strong.

ORCINUS ORCA

Either too tired themselves or having had their fill of mass and lip,
They discontinue with the chase, allow the blue whale the slip,
A great gaping mass of white blubber displayed, a battle wound,
Where it's dorsal once existed now nothing to be found.

Death is just hours away and the blue whale is now a beacon,
For sharks everywhere, more teeth, to be further stricken,
Sharks that keep clear of the killers, their unsavoury foe,
Unable to survive a fight against Orcinus they are in the know.

Orcinus orca is strong and resilient,
Feeds to fill, not to just kill, and so, honestly, quite lenient,
But practise its skills it does as any other,
All extremely intelligent, all mother, all brother.

SONG OF THE OCEAN

THE BIRTH

Orcas are one of the few animal species to have a distinct culture,
Hunting strategies occasionally unique, in many ways a rapture,
Cultural behaviours are learned, not clearly instinctive,
An individual initiates, others copy, seemingly meditative.

In the case of the seal hunting orcas, of Argentina most particular,
Orcas practice beaching and rescuing themselves until familiar,
Pass the skills on to their offspring in preparation,
Snatching seal pups from beaches, clear statement, no negation.

For thousands of years, before man recorded such an event,
Orcinus orca did hunt baleen whales, no remorse, no relent,
Each pod does seem to relish one meal over another,
Nothing here truly sacred, though enough facets to smother.

Of every ocean upon the planet,
Of all the time man cast to ocean his net,
Only once has it been witnessed,
And truly, with great respect, expressed.

Of the collaboration between beast and man,
For the harnessing of baleen, both meeting with plan,
Great prosperity, understanding and knowledge,
To hunt together, a silent and well endowed pledge.

ORCINUS ORCA

A family which went by the surname Davidson,
From them we peel back a great comparison,
Scrutinize the efforts of both, and we shall try and be blunt,
Where the killer, in accordance with need, did tax the human hunt.

Fresh meat, the flesh of the baleen,
Coated in oil so fresh and clean,
Source of income for man, meat for the killer whale,
Sheer oppression for baleen, for baleen sheer [archaic] bale.

Taking place at well-known Twofold Bay,
A particular pod of killers would return each year for short stay,
A bay near Eden on the Australian East Coast,
Such an extraordinary story unfolds, one in which to give toast.

This unwritten contract between man and whale stalker,
Evil man and the 'labelled unkindly' Orcinus orca,
This story of the killer is not meant to specifically qualify,
But of all understanding it does tend to superimpose and mystify.

It is a main jest of this story to reflect upon their character,
Give to each that owned, great stature,
Grasp here a true understanding and overall picture,
We start in the year 1862 and steer clear of giving lecture.

From a distance the dorsal of the killers can be seen,
To perforate the surface of the ocean, cutting clean,
Cutting effortlessly through the gentle rolling of each wave,
The road ahead soon to be set, ready to pave.

SONG OF THE OCEAN

Each of the mammals beneath are fully aware,
Flippers engaged, gliding through the ocean and sun's glare,
For they surface from time to time, now and again,
More often than not at same instance, similarity it does maintain.

The spouting of water seems the effect of the action,
Air ejected from the blowhole an immediate reaction,
It looks like that of a great cloud of mist,
Exploding from within, an action unable to resist.

Escaping air turning into water droplets, a voluminous sneeze,
Which dissipates in the air, carried away on the breeze,
Fresh breeze coming from the south, prepare for another dive,
By sucking in more oxygen, thriving, staying alive.

It is a wonder in itself to see such a mushrooming cloud,
Each erupting from within, power in which to be proud,
A peaceful cloud of beauty, so serene, one cannot ignore,
Unlike the cloud created by man and his inclination to war.

There is calm about it, no fragment of mind but something surreal,
Where one can become lost in a dream, a fantasy to steal,
Forget not this place in the world, an oyster's pearl,
Nothing like sitting back and watching the event unfurl.

But an even bigger event is about to unfold and take place,
Near land, in the tropics, close to Hawaii, waters of grace,
The pristine waters on which they now lay visit,
Worth all the time in the world to make this transit.

ORCINUS ORCA

A matriarch so young knows no better place to conclude this ride,
Other bays and inlets that she has visited, all brushed aside,
Her name to be Stranger and young at just 14 years,
Sexual maturity reached at 11 years, mature amongst peers.

Surrounded by members of her pod, an appeal to social science,
Other killer whales that had joined her in her adolescence,
Each seeing that she had purpose and great vision,
She knew of things that they did not, an apparition.

Stranger had been accepted as their matriarch without argument,
Setting themselves alongside for all to learn, behold this moment,
Even now, after the short, 16 months that they had been together,
Their dialect had transposed itself as different from any other.

Uniqueness unfolding with their traits as a unit,
Drawn together through conviction, drawn to a magnet,
She had fallen pregnant when with a large pod of 'offshore',
But departed that life, for she saw that the world held more.

And she departed alone,
Her mate holding heart of stone,
Male did remain with the pod he trusted and knew,
Stranger, now matriarch, of great vision she grew.

So now she has her own pod, her family,
Each joining her as though off assembly,
There was Typee, at 23 years, the oldest, stout, and lover,
He had a mate, whose dorsal was completely bent over.

SONG OF THE OCEAN

His mate was Humpy, 17 years, many more in store,
Had partnered with Typee several years before,
Typee having left his previous pod due to the death of his mother,
Of breeding age, you could not part them, eyes for one another.

There is also another pair to meet,
Two more, seemingly young, in which to greet,
The male is Cooper, the female named Big Ben in error,
Both 11 years of age and coupled years before, for their pleasure.

Cooper and Big Ben, dependent on one another,
It was their spirit as a couple, desire to be together,
Desire forcing them to separate from pod the previous year,
Inseparable, even during the hunt, always wanting to be near.

So here they were, a small pod of five,
To soon be swollen by one, beginning to thrive,
Stranger to give birth right here and now,
The beginning of an explosion to population, for them to grow.

For Stranger's abilities in the hunt would become legendary,
To all it was clear, clear and adverse to quandary,
Many male and female alike soon to join them,
Stranger the limb of which would grow many stem.

Little communication was shared between the member so near,
As they continued slowly on their way to waters so clear,
Patrolling waters, considered humanly far from shore,
No alert to prey on which to opportunistically impose much gore.

ORCINUS ORCA

For prey could be almost anywhere,
Could be here, could be there,
With a new mouth to feed coming their way,
They would remain, always, alert for new prey.

Searching constantly would be its own reward,
Whilst they waited the birth of their newest ward,
But stem that communication between each killer,
Which is a natural part of life, of their society a pillar.

Communication takes place during parts of the day or night,
Times that are more appropriate, to infringe a frightful blight,
Dialect modified over the decades, year to year,
Learnt and curved, for members of the pod all is clear.

Regional variations that are perfected,
Customized and never neglected,
Employed methodically without thought,
It is that which they now suppress, as taught.

This pod as for others are social,
With this there is nothing special,
And a small pod is more prone to seek company,
Even if such is human and unable to join in their symphony.

In this alone we find it hard to believe,
That creatures of the deep can feel, can grieve,
Or that they have a connection,
With the human race, of any description.

SONG OF THE OCEAN

They feel the effects of loneliness,
As well as overwhelming degrees of bliss,
They experience fear and embarrassment, I'm sure,
As men do, with their mistakes they do deplore.

But yet this is still far from their minds, present is a prize,
For a birth is taking place before their very eyes,
Tom delivered unto the world and vocalization can be heard,
Sound echoes out across the ocean, gliding, on wings of a bird.

The mother's abdomen is swollen with a foetus so large,
One that has been gestating for 17 months, the pods first charge,
Stranger swims around displaying some discomfort,
Her restless commotion drawing a little concern for effort.

She rises for breath, expelling mist, to atmosphere she gave,
Remaining there, just below each softening wave,
She can feel the soft breeze upon her skin,
The warmth did shine upon her, scene enough to draw a grin.

Her first born is about to make its way into the world,
She swims about and then suddenly pauses, her mind twirled,
Her flukes and head are lifted up, in sunlight, the glare,
Her back arched; she gives birth right then and there.

All other killers surround her, hearts happily torn,
Protecting her and the newborn,
Watching now their bated breath to be rewarded,
Of this newest member to the pod, to be well guided.

ORCINUS ORCA

Her thrashing about, which is necessary, visually learned,
Is natural and nothing in which to be concerned,
Somersaults and barrel rolls do aid, does not desist,
For good delivery one must be active, in pain, persist.

It is normal for the flukes to be seen first amidst ocean and sea,
Rarely the head, and the calf emerges to greet the glee,
And just a short period of delivery, for some a dramatic delight,
Delivery to reward the mother with greet reflection far from fright.

Tom is jettison delicately away from the mother of birth,
As Stranger gently accelerates forward and gives shallow girth,
The calf seen amidst red mist of blood from the torn umbilicus,
A sheen of gleam, shimmering, as though a form of mucus.

It dissipates as Tom now (if not clumsily) upwards does strive,
To surface just above, suck in his first lungful of air, to be alive,
Tom is born at last; the calf's triangle dorsal fin droops initially,
Fore flippers rigid, his flukes unfurl and thrashes deliberately.

Into the watery world in which he has been born,
Tom is free at last, to swim and splash about until worn,
To breathe the air above the surface of the ocean and to explore,
To have his heart filled with wondrous sights, more upon more.

He is lifted into the air on several occasions, seemingly ritualistic,
Much rubbing of skin on skin taking place, joyful, simplistic,
For all are overjoyed to see him born unto the world of serenity,
A little percussive activity takes place, never lacking in security.

SONG OF THE OCEAN

He will maintain a very close connection with his mother of birth,
For the first year of his life, and beyond, for what it is worth,
Grow of maturity, become stable, a part of the pod ever growing,
To be taught, looked after, escorted, to always be in the knowing.

Always to have other members of the pod on which to rely,
To be there, one for the other, now and in the by-and-by,
But the first year will see him in his mother's shadow,
To her whims and ways, to always be ready, to always bow.

Sheltered by her very body and flippers, his family,
Protected by her and pod in way most simile,
Provided good motherly support and sanction,
Pod ready to make secure by action.

But for the moment, the here and now, Stranger is a little tired,
Exhaustion dependant on delivery, though often feeling retired,
But happiness keeps her so optimistic and content,
Feeling of love so strong you can see it, from pores it does vent.

Tom now joins his mother to learn of this new life,
Away from comfort of womb: grow, kill, possibly find a wife,
So much now though to learn on the swim, forever more,
To breath, to learn the dialect and of the pods law.

They have much to be thankful for at present,
But Stranger is a little concerned, on pods safety spent,
For there is great safety in number and theirs is but few,
To see more killers within their pod would provide good view.

ORCINUS ORCA

A matriarch with great hunting ability and strategies to share,
She is worth her weight in gold: or should we say dietary fare,
Stranger recalled a place where blossoms could be looted,
A place where hunting whales could be recruited.

She had seen another pod in action,
One of similar interest and faction,
Had even shared with them the sport of the hunt,
Several orca she knew could be influenced, not to shunt.

She would recruit on Typee's aid for he was majestic and quick,
Good at hunting, good at killing, called to anger no short wick,
Grand at reading the thoughts of others, seemingly easy for him,
But he beheld one small factor which was requiring a slight trim.

He was too much of a commandeering sort in his nature,
Never to be made the leader of a sub-pod, to grow in stature,
But he did have abilities which she could milk, could bait,
Stranger reflected upon Typee's mate, Humpy, mind and state.

Humpy was a vicious type, by and large,
Not afraid to lead a head-on charge,
Not afraid to take a risk as may be the need,
Easy to manipulate and no need to plead.

Stranger would use her as a sub-pod contender for sure,
When the time was ripe Stranger would employ a lure,
But currently would allow Humpy to remain close by her side,
Yes, Stranger would have Humpy as an ally, along for the ride.

SONG OF THE OCEAN

This would keep Typee close and others even closer,
For those intimidated by Typee would remain all the tighter,
All would henceforth be subjected to Stranger, her road to win,
For the pod to grow in number and strength, currently too thin.

But there was plenty of time to reflect on tactics,
For now she was simply content with life and the basics,
To see Tom now swimming near her right flipper, just behind,
Searching for the retractable abdominal nipples, forever on mind.

And so he soon begins to suckle for the very first time,
Touch is sensitive, sometimes commanding but feeling, sublime,
Where a calf requests feeding from mother, a nourishing source,
Nudges, nibbles, fore-flipper caresses, feeding strategy, its course.

After some time at feeding Tom has had his fill, a great morsel,
He now precariously takes up position behind a fin, the dorsal,
To swim effortlessly along in the slipstream,
Tom is 8.2 feet long, weighs 200kg, a part of the team.

ORCINUS ORCA

THE BOATS OF GREEN

In the early Days and beyond a well-known fact did emerge,
Across the face of the whale-fishing industry, an interesting surge,
That seafaring vessels took in hand many different nationalities,
In particular South Sea Islanders, Aboriginals, for vast abilities.

As far as abilities go it must be spoken clearly, not to bork,
That for one reason or other some are called to particular work,
This is not racist or an attack on colour of skin but a wonder,
For some men are more apt at certain work, never to meander.

The Davidsons did learn this with the Yuin people,
A pillar of their enterprise at Twofold Bay, Eden, a steeple,
An industry set to harness that gift of the ocean to barrel,
Of New South Whales whaling, from small vessel most able.

Where can we find the town of Eden, one to come and love,
Near high cliffs that reach for the sky, so pretty at Snug Cove,
Close to the saddle and thereabouts, upon the plateau, the ground,
Quite picturesque and serine, of industry, the town can be found.

Eden does muse, to peer down at its harbour and over the bay,
Where a magnificent blue attracts, the eye upon to lay,
And sandy beaches of honeycomb break the line,
The line between ocean and forest surrounds, two to define.

SONG OF THE OCEAN

The lookout [Boyd tower on South Head] was badly damaged,
Never repaired, lightning in the 60's, its cursed, cruel passage,
But still put to good use for it could be seen across miles of ocean,
Served whalers well on occasion whilst upon waves of motion.

It was May of 1863 that George Davidson, of Eden was born,
This was his world, great pride and privilege to be worn,
Into the lap of one unmistakable scene, of which many were keen,
True semblance of a bay whaling station to be found, to be seen.

Two weatherboard homes found situated upon the bank,
Broad and strong, not limp or lank,
And near the bay an open shelter procured from wood,
A shelter waiting for whale blubber to be delivered as it should.

Beneath the shelter is where the brickwork of the try-works toil,
Large iron vats and large tanks for the storing of oil,
A windlass would see a whale carcass heaved with joy and hope,
To be hauled and deblubbered by way of a large rope.

The whaling station also consisted of long ramp,
Those iron vats just spoke with vast array of oil lamp,
Changed little for the entire time in operation,
This great opportunity, this small whaling station.

It was here they would haul the quantities of blubber into position,
Blubber from which to extract the oil from vast lesion,
9-inch strips of fat are ripped from the carcass beneath,
All that remains: a shell of red and pools of blood from death.

ORCINUS ORCA

Hope for good quantity,
Mandatory quality,
Hope for many hours of work,
Work hard, never to shirk.

Even when George was crawling on knees and hand,
He had become familiar with the boat house, where it did stand,
Where the shelter of 15 x 40 feet secured the boats,
To venture upon rolling waves, developing industrial moats.

The boats are shallow, carry a handful, are 29 feet long,
Sturdy and ready for rowing over waves so boisterous and strong,
Prepared for launch at a moment's notice, awaiting call to action,
Sitting, vacant the crew to power them over turbulence of ocean.

His grandfather, Set upon his way, Alexander Walker Davidson,
A Presbyterian treating everyone fairly, no matter the season,
Including the indigenous crews, hired and paid with a full wage,
Never to speak poorly of them, no pretence, no false stage.

He built a home from the wreck of the Lawrence Frost,
Along with a boatshed and workshop at little cost,
And for purpose at extracting information on the ship above,
We must extravagate a little for the added dimension we love.

The Lawrence Frost was a 1523 tonne ship made of timber,
Did not last long in life so clearly not sturdy but too limber,
Built in 1854 and sinking in 1856 would you believe,
Such a short life the owner could only grieve.

SONG OF THE OCEAN

Having been severely damaged during voyage to Australia,
In August of 1856 it did run ashore, solid ground, a qualia,
Seemingly carrying more tonnage than for which it was built,
We must wonder if the owner or captain did feel any guilt.

    But of this story we must, to history turn,
    At least a little of this we must learn,
    The ship was a mile from shore,
    The stopper to anchor seemingly tore.

It was having sail shortened, men putting to work, to rope,
With strong northerly wind and flood tide, they lost all hope,
The anchor let out 45 fathom of cable, had given way,
Then the second anchor, no strength to remain, no safely to stay.

To stay on ocean, upon the wave, the vessel would not behave,
No hope at all, of all her strength, she already gave,
Gave all hope to the churning of wave, wind, and ocean,
Dragged along with both anchors, floating, free of notion.

    Soon grounded hard ashore,
    Harsh breeze increasing all the more,
    Now a heavy ocean amidst strong gale,
    Pumps not good enough, no big enough pail.

    Ocean breaking clean over vessel,
    Toiled in wind like curtain tassel,
    The hold both fore and aft under siege,
    The encumbering waves, the ocean but their liege.

ORCINUS ORCA

All gone but still remembered, not truly lost in storm and rain,
Soon raised and repaired, to be up and running, set out again,
And now heading south after having taken trip to port in north,
She ran aground upon a spit, Twofold Bay, for what it is worth.

Set upon again by strong gale,
Bitter sweet its life, it did fail,
Driven to bay bed, not risen again to serve,
On second sinking, shattered completely, it had lost all nerve.

Washing aground near future whaling station to be,
Born of this wreckage, a family true, to work with glee,
The Lawrence Frost was condemned for all time,
But its body was recycled, to recall amidst berhyme.

Near the Kiah Inlet so small, positioned on the Towamba River,
1.6 miles across from town of Eden, employment to deliver,
On extreme side of the bay, away from mainstream bustle of life,
Many men came to work, not to drink heavily nor cause strife.

Varieties of crew stationed at Twofold Bay at one time or another,
Including the Barclay, Rixon, and the Walker [all brother],
The Whelan, Power and Newland,
Many names here as you can see, all come to make a stand.

But of all the men and boats that were cast into the ocean,
In an effort to kill a whale, the great devouring, a great action,
It was the Davidsons that had secured the majority of assistance,
From the killers directly, neither afraid to close their distance.

SONG OF THE OCEAN

For Orcinus disliked the explosive harpoons, the great noise,
The devilish weapon of some crews, employed without poise,
When hunting baleen, no mercy for the behemoth of biology,
The Davidsons held little interest for this modern technology.

This favouritism seemed to infuriate the other crews ever more,
To such a degree that more artillery came into play from store,
Which saw to it that the killers assisted the Davidsons only,
Their green boats identified as worthy: not corrupt, not phony.

The green was based on the traditional Scottish Davidson tartan,
Each the same colour, worn with pride, like the shield of a spartan,
Not to mention the silhouettes, faces, and characteristics,
Coming to know so well, their mannerisms, their basics.

Davidson, his small band of five boats, of the whole, each a tiller,
Securing an ally for all time, winning the assistance of the killer,
All others being ignored by the black and white Wolves of the Sea,
A great, tremendous fortune falling upon Davidson with glee.

Great favour to shine upon the Davidsons, to be bestowed,
For right whales were declining in number, they rarely showed,
In tune with the culmination of the hunt for the sperm whale,
A decline stemming from Tasmania from 1841, supply to fail.

Learning was a two-way street, of society a steeple,
Not just with Orcinus but also with people,
Indigenous crews offered Alexander advice, he taking notice,
Understand the Law of the Tongue and putting it into practise.

ORCINUS ORCA

In payment for the aid in catching the baleen each trip,
Killers were permitted to sup on the tongue and lip,
Greatest morsel of all that was caught,
Great delicacies which the killers always sought.

And not long into the strategies, forever aided, never coerced,
Familiarity did spring into thought, patterns to memory a nurse,
For dorsal fin and body markings were rather unique,
And as time passed by, each killer identified, names to speak.

Bay whalers found individual killers identity easy to diagnose,
Names derived from the Yuin deceased, now to disclose,
Tom, Hooky, Humpy, Jackson, Charlie, Typee,
Stranger, Montague, Old Ben, Young Ben, Sharkey.

Jimmy, Brierly, Walker, Kinscher, Youngster,
Skinner, Big Jack, and Little Jack, Cooper,
But incorrect identity did occasionally occur via the dorsal tail,
Some names are placed in error, both for female and male.

Many others remain unspoken for there are too many to quote,
Around 50 killers amongst three pods, often hard to keep note,
Each pod, in some cases, again split into smaller,
Sub-pods of varied size, no records to enlighten us further.

It was truly amazing how the killers would cooperate,
Not just with each other, but the Davidsons first rate,
In a concert of manipulation, and well-tuned, to orchestrate,
Tendered manoeuvres, a military juggernaut, precision spate.

SONG OF THE OCEAN

Pods would attend their assigned choir, aligned and tasked,
Going through its paces, happily doing as was asked,
One pod positioning itself out to ocean to prevent escape,
To drive a baleen in towards the coast, of life to rape.

Another would cut off any escape to North,
Of the whales migratory route for what it is worth,
The third would hone in, attack, harass the prey,
In some cases this could take almost all day.

But a day of light,
Did not sourly bite,
Far worse could this be in getting food to table,
If no aid from whalers was made available.

So pleasurable it was to be working well together,
So seldom met was this deliverance, good standing, good tether,
As offered by the skilful throwing, most stoutly, of harpoon,
And lance from the bay whalers, driving it home, never too soon.

The poor baleen had no way of escape, no way out,
Even unable to dive, so painful it was, even unable to shout,
Running short on energy, unable to move or break loose,
May as well consider, already, flukes to capstan and noose.

For killers would surround their prey, approach from all side,
As well as from below, forever to torment, to ride and ride,
To throw themselves upon the baleen's back, so soul breaking,
An attempt to smother its blowhole, restrict its breathing.

ORCINUS ORCA

Each year the killer whales moved from their Antarctic station,
To the coast of East Australia, tempering a weather negation,
Following the deadly breeze of winter as it maintained approach,
The streamlined move of baleen, swimming, ready to poach.

The winter months, a move into waters much warmer,
Not considered common amongst all pods, quite dissimilar,
For many remained stationed where food was more stable,
But the killers of Twofold Bay learnt to self-aid where able.

Here they lay, just off the coast, not that easily found,
In wait for prey as they made for their breeding/feeding ground,
Rarely far from shore,
An easy kill, an easy score.

For the migratory routes of the baleen brought the great whales,
Along the coastline, as fodder upon sheep fields, hay in bales,
Past Leather Jacket Bay and where it lay,
and then on towards Eden, Twofold Bay.

It was at Leather Jacket that the killers sprung their ambush,
In an attack of several phases, ready to push and push,
The prowling killer, on the loose, searching for his food,
There he was, always hungry, always in that mood.

The sperm whale fed mainly on diet of octopus,
The dolphin upon fish without fuss as did the grampus,
But the black and white of their close relation,
Fed upon them and grampus, great souls of this watery nation.

SONG OF THE OCEAN

Whale was their tender choice, lip and tongue, a meal, a snack,
But mostly the killer whale was after the humpback,
But lacked much interest in the fin whale and blue for the present,
Both faster in the water, too much energy in the catch hence spent.

Certainly too fast for the rowing power of the men of Eden,
Unless aided by a pull on the ropes, attached, a boat so laden,
An easier kill was much preferred over hard,
No risk in over doing it, forced to retard.

This was the pods way, their chosen path, higher food estimate,
Some pods chose to remain in a much colder climate,
A minority preferred the warmer,
But all chose to occupy large areas to wander.

With purpose written upon face of one region compared to next,
Common sense factors associated with each in context,
If a particular fish is unavailable, cycle-of-life getting the better,
Then reason there is for diet or scenery change, no need to fetter.

For preference is always given to survival,
In particular to the young, being more temperamental,
So it was here that the killers had congregated,
Extremely fast to react and executed, their time well slated.

Watching as the identities of those beneath, their dorsal glide,
Effortlessly through the water, to unceasing pressures they abide,
Higher up, Tom with his mark and Hooky with his,
Distinguishing well, one from the other, hard to miss.

ORCINUS ORCA

The pod makes its way to the grounds to feed,
Their home for the winter months ahead, to fill their need,
The matriarch has made her choice,
Given command, raised her voice.

Initially the pods are split, one a mile out from coast,
Another at two miles, and a third at three, at most,
Set upon an angle in order to channel their prey,
Towards the shore, a path of upheaval to lay.

And so a baleen is seen,
Not at all a smear or lean,
Not strange, a pregnant whale,
By herself, unaided, no male.

It is now, we see them dispatch two of their own,
Towards Twofold Bay where to them, unbeknown,
A lookout is positioned at Boyd tower on South Head,
Awaiting sign from the killer whale, awaiting sign to be read.

Here the crews of Davidson's boats will soon launch,
There so waiting with glee, mercilessly staunch,
When, soon to unveil, a cow and unborn calf to make appearance,
Heading northward and into the trap of pure nuisance.

On seeing in moonlight the spurts of a whale in due course,
The lookout at Boyd Tower would take to his horse,
Ride at a great pace the 2.5 miles to the Kiah Inlet,
Only to find that Tom's call had already been met.

SONG OF THE OCEAN

Tom the killer, the best of the Orcinus, in more cases than not,
Swam to the mouth of the River, the best delivery spot,
Where the Davidsons were housed in two isolated buildings,
So constructed for life and leisure, their pleasure and feelings.

From within the bay Tom commenced upon his calling alert,
Calling the men ashore to act, with harpoon and lance, the expert,
Flop-tailing until the whalers made their way into the water,
Waters of the bay, aboard boats, to awaiting escort and slaughter.

Yes, flop-tailing, for the Davidsons alone, dropping hint, a clue,
Such visitation seen nowhere else upon the globe, this is true,
Tom and Hooky, seemingly acting as a sub-pod now detached,
Lead boats out to weary and tired baleen, for it to be dispatched.

The glowing bioluminescent trail they followed, this crew,
The stark morning light aided by moon, little light it threw,
It was to become fate, therefore, that Tom would become,
The most recognisable of all the killers, and sight most welcome.

Tom's regular contact with the men saw to it quite plainly,
That their trusting relationship did grow astoundingly,
Regardless of his sometimes annoying and playful nature,
Their working together was somewhat of a national feature.

The harpoon is thrown hard and it sticks fast,
HOORAH! bellows out for all to hear to the last,
For the whale has been stuck well, the bite does well adhere,
The unborn calf moving inside her now never to appear.

ORCINUS ORCA

The mother fears for her young,
Holes within her, much blood sprung,
The baleen's presence of mind now clear to the killers,
And the killers like what they register, the stoutest millers.

And now the fear grows ever strong within the humpback,
It is her own undoing, courage she does now lack,
STERN ALL! then becomes clear and the boat is dragged,
All oars pulled in unison with great strength, cow almost bagged.

Oars are pulled back in order to help slow the leviathan,
It is part and parcel of the courage and plan,
The cow then tries to escape from the threat, an attempt to purge,
The whale turns abruptly and water begins to abruptly surge.

One of the boats is bobbing about upon the waves of the ocean,
And the turbulence of the fight is easy to see in its motion,
The boat is pointed at both ends, built for the stresses of the fight,
Built for momentum forward and aft, not in order to take flight.

Made of good cedar and built to last,
To ride out the ocean waves so vast,
But few can handle the thrashing of flukes now no longer mute,
The thrashing of a whale gone mad, it is in a wild dispute.

With the misfortune of a capsized boat, men will shout out,
The killers would assist, happily, freely, to give tout,
Tom now with the charged duty of ensuring their safety was keen,
Swimming around the boat's crew, protecting, it has to be seen.

SONG OF THE OCEAN

Great assistance here in the commotion of the fight,
Battle against the whale, using fluke, no teeth to bite,
Men would struggle to stay afloat in rough ocean or seas,
Having pulled out of Twofold Bay, their desire to please.

Tom was truly a member of the family,
A friendship so strange but trusted heavily,
Such damage to boats was seen often,
But to the men's spirit it does never soften.

Tom lifted all of their spirit,
Had to be gifted with great merit,
And now the baleen continues with last effort to survive,
Now last, huge effort, for her and unborn to stay alive.

But the attackers concerted efforts won out,
Much pleasure in victory to shout,
Their maintenance of boats kept in-house,
Tended to like wife, like spouse.

Boats made to last, Alexander's son, John, helping with carpentry,
No easy skill, not to purchase from shop and place in pantry,
With their combined skill, and boats so sturdily built,
A great victory with Orcinus, towering high, not so easily tilt.

ORCINUS ORCA

THE HUNT

George Davidson in 1877, 14 years of age, soon to take stage,
Upon his own whaling journey, ready to turn the page,
By picking up the struggle against the ocean, a fight to ever last,
And sperm whaling was considered by many as a thing of the past.

The whaling industry in general was brutal,
Had proved, for the sperm whale, to be fatal,
Slaughtered to near extinction,
An arbitrary stemming of life and eviction.

George wasn't tall in stature but was to become respected,
Amongst his peers and others far away seemingly celebrated,
For many, many reasons, to be toasted as a man, most remarkable,
To be placed within the annals of history, most able, most stable.

But for now we see a boy turning into a man of renown,
Mature and serious, and occasionally, as with all men, a clown,
His strengths were both hard and easy to see,
All he could do was dream of what was soon to be his reality.

He had a spring in his step, one to procure a smile and a stare,
Walked with arms swinging as though without a care,
Confident but certainly never cocky or juvenile,
Being more than he was; no, no, an utter denial.

SONG OF THE OCEAN

He bore a distinctive arch upon his nose,
His eyes were a clear blue, tranquil, full of repose,
Most remarkable and seemingly hypnotising,
Though in a friendly way, to some were astonishing.

He wished to be a whaler,
Like his father, whale hauler,
And his wish was about to become true,
Right, humpback, and blue.

He watched from upon a hill, steadily firm and well perched,
As the men battled against a leviathan of the ocean as it lurched,
Gaining ground on whale, most remarkable, something to learn,
George, utterly astounded, to a great degree, never to spurn.

My God! how the killers felt the prolonged urge to feed,
This overwhelming encouragement and requirement, or need,
Not just food but to lay visit upon Twofold Bay,
Every year, one after the next, upon these quarters to lay.

Not missing a single season,
Not for any known reason,
They always came, to this place they returned,
Like a gathering of children, compulsion within them burned.

As though drawn to their place of birth,
A place keenly sought, this heaven on Earth,
But even with their exceptional hearing, within their surrounds,
It came to pass, occasional feed was missed within their grounds.

ORCINUS ORCA

But were they missed or is that an incorrect view,
For man has little idea of their mannerisms, no real clue,
For more to the point the Orcinus is making a decision,
On which whale to attack, being more precise in their precision.

Scenarios had to be measured and food secured,
Always a preference on which prey should be lured,
From mans' perspective the situation was visibly shallow,
For it was they who failed in seeing source, advantage and tallow.

The Davidson's would hit the surface of the water to alert,
Orca to presence of humpback, though Orcinus was the expert,
Of their current position and need for support on the spot,
Killers turning in unison, either accept the ultimatum or not.

For it would save them much time in bringing down a whale,
Even if less worthy, much easier sport to wrap as in bale,
With the aid of men in boats, their harpoon and lance,
Regardless of their strategic position at a glance.

Tom could see, feel and hear,
The other killers around him, so near,
Those of the pod in which he did belong,
The pod commanded by Humpy, powerful and strong.

Humpy commanded over the pod with extreme precision,
Courtesy and steadfast will to procure good decision,
Leading by example and displaying a great understanding,
Of those within her pod and of the meal they were landing.

SONG OF THE OCEAN

But before the formalities of the hunt could take place,
They were to be joined once more by Stranger as she made pace,
The two pods to join in the hunt as one,
Ceremony to prelude, from matriarch upon throne.

A ceremony that occurred from time to time, a must,
When a number of pods, of related killers, did readjust,
Joined back together after a degree of absence,
Having gone their separate ways in forage, now in their presence.

The two pods were lined abreast, opposite each other,
Facing off, preparing to be joined again as though lost lover,
Slowly but surely both groups do approach,
Drawing closer, closing the gap, no rehearsal, no coach.

They were now at 65 feet apart when they came to a halt,
Sounding delicately their calls, to habituate, secure by bolt,
Looking upon one another over the space between,
Seeing all, hearing all, temperate in pleasure, tapered clean.

After half a minute of ceremonial action,
Swimming together, again strong faction,
Submerged and surfaced shortly after, mingling again,
They were now ready for the hunt, unable to refrain.

Now the pods of strengthened unity make their move,
Towards Eden and Twofold Bay, in the groove,
For they can hear the movement of the whale,
Soon to find themselves in the fight, hard on tail.

ORCINUS ORCA

The baleen, will however, put up a grand resistance,
Stubborn and worthy, the only victory, pure persistence,
From time to time the killers of the pod would vacate,
Vacate from watery surrounds to pressure and berate.

What do we mean by vacate and berate, what is this tale?
They leap from water, propel themselves upon back of whale,
To cover its blowhole, prevent it breathing, for it to drown,
Forcing the beast to suffocate, meal secured, life put down.

The whale would usually try to then dive, to avoid all grief,
But its efforts to do so would be thwarted by killers beneath,
Then another animal suddenly shoots itself out of the water,
In order to block the blowhole, its life now the shorter.

A gasp for air in the build-up of fear is denied,
For pregnant humpback, ample air supply is no longer supplied,
The humpback is heavily flanked,
Life expectancy not highly ranked.

Some orca head to the front, slow the escape, aid with the capture,
A concerted effort by all, a lengthy battle to butcher, their nature,
None will go without a meal, the youngest being fed first,
Hunger for blubber, for blood, that thirst for the win the worst.

The stress within the humpback mounts but doesn't peak,
It just keeps on growing, smell of fear to leak,
Thoughts falling upon the unborn calf that she carries within,
Carried for 11 months, two weeks, on verge of birth and grin.

SONG OF THE OCEAN

She had departed, some time ago, the waters of the Antarctic,
Made for traditional breeding grounds, to find something tragic,
It is so obvious to this humpback, crying for condolement,
That there will be no solace from the predicament.

The humpback's concern now was for the safety of her unborn,
Nothing but cloak of terror to now, until death, be worn,
Her song-like choruses soon to be none, gone such purity,
And the birthing of calf never to be that joyous reality.

A killer made another strike upon her, being now so frail,
Her 39 foot length from head to fluke, the powerful tail,
Another chunk of blubber being taken from her side,
The pain searing, shooting through body, nowhere to hide.

What had she done to deserve such torment before death,
Was her unborn already dead, no longer to inhale that first breath?
She shook the thought from her mind, complete and utter denial,
To seek the only option open... complete and utter survival.

She wished to live, be free, to feed again, satisfaction to feel,
Her diet of capelin, herring, mackerel, and sand lance [sand eel],
To swim with mouth open, baleen plates delivering her meal,
To take as needed, plenty for all, no such thing as to steal.

Never to feel fish against 380 baleen plates as they stack,
The comb-like plates covered in a series of bristles, olive-black,
To feel the warmth of a full stomach; no, never more to know,
If she didn't fight now there would be no food, no tomorrow.

ORCINUS ORCA

At the present all she could see was death as it teased,
Regardless of this a great surge of power within released,
Now fighting most heroically: her life, to self, now appealed,
Gone were all negative thought, her fate shall not be sealed.

And it is now that the bay whalers appear,
To aid in the killing of the humpback so near,
Providing assistance, and vice-versa, to the pods,
Orcinus in agreement, spy-hopping with nods.

Neither was disappointed with this alliance,
Quick in their decision and action, shared reliance,
Despite the killers being near exhausted,
Much more delivery of hatred must be sported.

The harpooner exchanges places with the headsman real fast,
As quickly as possible can be in small boat on ocean so vast,
The headsman positioned himself and readied himself with lance,
For the killing to continue, many hours of labour seen at a glance.

The cold of the night to be endured, the thirst: and the rapture,
The torn muscles and sore throat endured in effort to capture,
And with the concerted efforts of gigantic proportion,
The activity became hectic, of time they had no notion.

Tom would quite often be seen to jostle with the rope,
Already fastened to a harpoon, gifting men much hope,
Tom enjoying himself more than ever before,
A comical occurrence and sight to see for ever more.

SONG OF THE OCEAN

Hanging onto the harpoon line for up to 30 minutes he did,
Being dragged by the force of the humpback, for survival it bid,
Swimming through surging ocean which grew and then subsided,
Tom being dragged along like a dead weight, effortlessly glided.

Tom was being pulled upon the surface of the ocean with glee,
He did this by biting upon the rope, in his mouth, all could see,
Or simply placing the rope beneath one of his flippers so strong,
Tom, a mature animal or not, in this action saw no wrong.

The battle continues well into the night,
Lances thrown with great effort, during the fight,
To be placed between the ribs of the whale not easily found,
To penetrate deep and cause that inflicting, deadly wound.

An incorrect placement of lance would see the effort wasted,
For little damage may be done, no victory to be tasted,
Or the lance might simply fall out and sink to the ocean floor,
Equipment lost forever, never retrieved, employed never more.

The moon then showed itself, and with sudden realisation,
A great commotion and vision, a great sensation,
Men stand, cheer, blood now rushing from blowhole most clear,
A sign that the kill, that victory, was so very near.

With this the whale suddenly commences with its death flurry,
Death now certain, vision blurring, no longer any need to worry,
The end is nigh, the humpback has no doubt,
With spraying of blood from blowhole, last of life gives sprout.

ORCINUS ORCA

And the joy of the win is exuberating,
This to say the least, worthy of celebrating,
The men commence about the task of attaching buoy and anchor,
To secure the kill, an action adhered to, always a factor.

The Orcinus move in for their prize of the fight,
Forcing the humpback's mouth open, to tear and to bite,
Forcing their way into where the tongue sits ready,
Body of whale now unmoving, limp and most steady.

Calves are fed first and then those that remain most gratefully,
None taking more than they should; all is shared equally,
The tongue to soon be devoured completely, hunger gone, beaten,
Lips soon fed upon, appetising, very little left, almost all is eaten.

By the time the first of the killers has fed on this bulky shape,
Others further out to ocean, protecting flanks, preventing escape,
Move in and take what is for them and nothing more,
Having done their duty, keeping the whale close to shore.

The pods depart and leave all alone,
Now for the men to strip to the bone,
But not just yet, later the blubber can be dispatched,
At present they ensure the anchor is well attached.

The crew now returns home, to rest from work, not fun,
To claim the carcass later on, amidst light from sun,
When the gases of putrefaction goes to work upon this prize,
Around 24 hours after the sinking with anchor, it will rise.

SONG OF THE OCEAN

And the killers below, both adult and nippers,
Finish feeding upon head, flukes and flippers,
The whale on ocean floor away from swelling and turbulence,
To be exhumed when gases provide that essential deliverance.

Yes; that's what George saw, without a mistake,
Looking over the bay, the scene unfold and end, in mind to bake,
Many more dreams by day of what he saw to his front,
One day, he, ready upon boat, hard work delivered with a grunt.

ORCINUS ORCA

THE AGREEMENT

Two boats spearheaded towards the open water, easy to see,
Heading towards the entrance of the bay, wind to lee,
Competing for the prize that they had to have,
For oil from whale, for families sustenance, for poorer to stave.

The years did not favour too many partnerships competing,
Not for the same, right, humpback fin or blue, to be stripping,
Stripping blubber from carcass as turbulent times bided,
And the arduous competition at Eden slowly subsided.

The Davidson's vision to be the only whalers of the bay,
To grow and outlast, come of fruition, before them to lay,
But for present each boat surged forward, shoulders rolling,
Oars in hands, five oars apiece, amidst much friendly berating.

But the harpooner of Davidson's crew was already of mind,
To spring from position, desertion with pride,
To take his post with his thigh placed in the concave of his thwart,
To ready with a harpoon in hand, just as he was taught.

There was a great spout of water erupting from the surface,
A right whale had most temporarily shown a face of grimace,
Water foaming for an instant and the surface being disrupted,
By the gigantic lifting of flukes, ever dangerous, never disputed.

SONG OF THE OCEAN

The tail then disappearing back into the ocean, dark as death,
Diving once more after having replenished its resourceful breath,
Seconds later the unmistakable dorsal of Tom was there,
Having erupted from the water, for his magnificence to be bear.

His entire body lifted out and seemed to freeze,
For just a second, in mid-air, amidst the strong breeze,
It was like a holy man witnessing a true vision afore,
A religious treat, a great specimen, there to adore.

Big Jack was alongside Tom and now headed to his port,
Endeavouring to cut off the right whale's dive, a last resort,
For no good it would do in the harbour of Twofold Bay,
For it was not that deep, the right had no chance this day.

But Big Jack was also aware of a possible retreat to be gained,
From beneath the waves where harpoon and lances now refrained,
Of those upon the boat, they could not see nor reach,
Not for love of money, seated here or from position on beach.

George could be seen, his silhouette upon a hill,
Overlooking the cliff where he stood, feeling the thrill,
Watching as the two crews thrashing at the ocean, sweated it out,
With all their strength, giving commands, many orders to shout.

They were trying with all their power to be the first,
Within distance of the whale, to quench their thirst,
To hurtle a harpoon against that great mass all knew,
The whale that had temporarily disappeared from view.

ORCINUS ORCA

It was George's dad, John Davidson, his jet-black beard,
Much hair on face, his commands direct and calmly steered,
It was his boat against another, a boat manned by Bob Love,
Competition between each too fierce: two hands, one glove.

The screwed up looks upon their faces told the story,
And their every muscle tore at the oars for glory,
This was the fight of champions, the fight for 'fast fish',
The rule, securing rights to whale, each could only pray and wish.

The ocean was choppy and breeze strong, no real restriction,
The freshness doing little to upset the situation,
But the work was still hard enough,
You had to be extremely tough.

And as the oars continued to beat at the ocean,
From within the security of the row-locks of little friction,
Only time to stroke and stroke, to get ahead,
To pierce the body of whale with iron needle and rope for thread.

Davidson was making more ground than Love,
That extra asserted effort and seemingly praised from high above,
John looked behind him to realise the headway they had gained,
Seeing his men give no quarter, from hard work, never refrained.

He could see the sun as it set behind the bulk of Mount Imlay,
The sun quitting its quarters having given up its stay,
And a strong feeling of wholeness penetrated his soul,
His home, gentle surf plunging within the bay, this watery bowl.

SONG OF THE OCEAN

It was home, upon the rocks at the foot of high cliff,
Where the swells of undulating ocean moved, constant riff,
The gentle waves caressing, music to ear so grand,
Long waves of white breaking upon the sand.

Long waves of white water broke along Whale Spit,
An elongated portion of beach, close to land was knit,
Debris of the Lawrence Frost still sticking up here and there,
Two white cottages glancing down as though to stare.

And the fight beneath the waves continued unabated,
To prevent the right from escaping to ocean, not related,
The right whale different in many ways and aspect,
Nothing here to truly decipher nor inspect.

The right whale was to endeavour,
To attempt the impossible, nothing in favour,
For even if he escaped to ocean and open water,
The other pods of killers were ready to slaughter.

Tom then abandoned his manoeuvre and raced to the surface,
The whale changing direction, tempers burning like furnace,
Both Big Jack and Humpy made the effort now to impede,
To act deliberately and with great speed.

Tom broke the surface and half turned,
Crashing down upon his flank, surface of ocean churned,
Turning to face the crew of the green boat,
He looked upon them momentarily as though to gloat.

ORCINUS ORCA

He was trying to gain their attention, the headsman, John,
John saw then what was to play before his eyes, before gone,
He had seen Tom do this before but could not clarify,
What it was that was passing between them, but do not deny.

Tom seemed to look at him directly in the eyes,
Communicating his dire need, no hidden ties,
Tom then turned into the choppy waves and sped off, to tear,
Leading boat to whale's next surface, he requiring a breath of air.

Tom was showing them the way,
John saw all the cards fall into place, there to lay,
The connection between Tom's antics of the past,
The commotion now performed, every move, down to the last.

They were being escorted, pure and simple, from the front,
Shown the way as any usher would do, this was not a stunt,
Tom wished nothing more than to assist as best he could,
In the demise of the right whale, together, as they should.

Tom could easily see the dark flesh of Sam, he stood out,
He knew then that the harpoon would fly with encouraging shout,
For Sam placed his oar, opposite the thole-pins, into socket,
Harpoon then picked up, position sought, to throw like rocket.

He barely had time to place the weapon upon his right shoulder,
A grasp taken upon the shaft of iron, strong grasp of the holder,
The whale then surfaced briefly as Tom veered to the right,
Between the killer and the crew, and it was a beautiful sight.

SONG OF THE OCEAN

Sam hurtled the harpoon forward and down, no mere morsel,
Into the fatty layer and penetrating deep beneath the dorsal,
The whale lunged forward with a suddenness expected,
Much water splashing over the crew but work never neglected.

They pulled back on the oars in tune, not too late, not too soon,
The manila rope holding tight, most secure to the harpoon,
The line was tight but able to run freely through the loggerhead,
Running smoothly, unrestricted, through eye of needle so thread.

All oars were now quickly peaked for good reason,
Pulled from the water in hurried unison,
Secured into position and out of harm's way,
Well clear of the surface of the ocean, there to stay.

The ocean could snap an oar instantly,
Like a toothpick and quite neatly,
To deliver against body a great wretchedness lacking negation,
Against flesh and bone, crippling crew beyond expectation.

The right whale thrashed mightily, dived, feeling stress,
The boat surging forward under great duress,
John manipulating the sweep in a manner of grasp and control,
Watching the right, the surge of the ocean, it beginning to take toll.

As carefully as one could he considered all possibility,
Watching for when the whale may turn quite unexpectedly,
For that dreaded moment when the whale might turn,
Capsize the boat with thundering power, he could never spurn.

ORCINUS ORCA

Tom looked back again, seeing the harpoon stuck fast,
Considered for a brief moment the other crew, no prize for last,
Bob Love continued, hoping for harpoon to shudder and shake,
That the right whale might surface, for the hook's hold to break.

John stood, Sam and he to exchange position right now,
Sam taking up the sweep and John moving to the bow,
The commencement of the right whale's milling,
To ready the lances for the actual killing.

Tom reacted, dove beneath, to continue with his achievement,
Where Humpy and Big Jack commenced with their harassment,
No prolonged diving nor heading out to ocean permitted,
To be turned to the surface, movement to be restricted.

They surged out of the water and upon the whale's back,
Trying with all their might to cover the blowhole, their attack,
Breathing now harder to perform, no longer available,
To hurry the arrival of death, to draw good air, no longer able.

The first lance was then expertly thrown, a throw to last,
It penetrating deep, between the ribs, sticking fast,
exactly where it was aimed as good as any could throw,
The right whale moving in circles, absurdly nowhere to go.

Taking the boat and its crew with him, he swam wildly,
John throwing another lance which also hit its mark most tidily,
And within minutes a spout of red erupted from the blowhole,
A short dive and the whale was dead, Orcinus to take their toll.

SONG OF THE OCEAN

John saw, as the others did, the orca move fast and without fail,
They in turn quick to set buoy and anchor to whale,
To set it adrift, to sink to the sandy floor,
Where killers could have their fill of lips and more.

Gases would see the whale afloat in a day or two,
To then be collected for deblubbering, a task they knew,
And so both Orcinus and men were pleased,
Each getting the gift they wished, their needs appeased.

The call was made to pod out to ocean, their cordon, their shield,
They came thundering in for their part of the yield,
Where each and every one of them would get their share,
None more than another, all equal, always fair.

There was more to come in the following days and many a week,
With or without the help of the Davidson's, a season yet to peak,
Though the help was a benefit to the killers, strategically rated,
For their energy reserves would then not be so depleted.

Stranger watched over the feeding, upon it she would glare,
Ensuring that none took more than their fair share,
But greed wasn't something in a killer to easily find,
Wasn't even a contemplation of mind.

These mammals were family, they were one and the same,
Of the same pod, of the same line, minds of similar frame,
They owed one another more than any man could realise,
For each one acted freely and willingly, each seemingly wise.

ORCINUS ORCA

Sure, they were each an individual, one and all,
But never alone, part of a team, a pyramid so tall,
Their pod: their religion, true faith and miracle,
Everything to them, from base to pinnacle.

Humpy was looked upon as a strong and powerful pod leader,
Stranger knew her well, felt attached, by measure a pilaster,
She also looked effectively at both Tom and Hooky,
Of Hooky we have not spoken, hauntingly beautiful, not spooky.

Hooky was Stranger's second son,
Of his father, of information, I have none,
For there is little to say of this thing,
Of a mid-Antarctic ocean fling.

Animals may act as much for self, as they do for the group,
For pod: in this we should not deeply delve [archaic] stoop,
For to search for ever and a day, needle in stack of hay,
We may find it hard to understand customs as they lay.

But to employ a stranger for her need,
Not for selfishness or for greed,
Possibly still an animal instinct and the need to feed,
We shall not speak of whether from her own pod she did breed.

To uphold her splendidness,
To maintain her vision of boldness,
To assume her great effectiveness,
To always, in her, behold trustworthiness.

SONG OF THE OCEAN

Hooky was male, as per Tom, and only a little younger,
Born of a father whom shall always remain a stranger,
And Stranger preferred it this way,
Fathers of whom would have no future sway.

Her faction is currently strong in number,
But split into pods and segregated by much water,
They saw little of one another when hunting,
They all knew they were of the same bunting.

Favourites: necessary to ensure longevity, and Stranger did have,
Kept them close, under sway, moving forward, a way to pave,
Typee, Humpy, Cooper, Big Ben, Tom, Hooky and Big Jack,
All loved, all grand and worthy, through seasons as they stack.

Each of them knew the men aboard the boats of green,
All capable of working with them, all very keen,
But for now they swam 1.9 miles south for Leather Jacket Bay,
Thirty members strong, for a short rest, for a short stay.

ORCINUS ORCA

THE MINKE

George's task, at the beginning of his long and rewarding career,
Rewarded by its love, equation of money did not appear,
Was to assist his Uncle Jim upon the lookout,
One of square shape and footing, the ocean all about.

Of where do we speak? Well it is close,
Leased by his father, and good advantage rose,
All the land leased in fact, from South Head to Towamba River,
Great advantage over competitor, worth far more than a stiver.

Not only did he have the best post,
From which to look for whale-sign the most,
But the killers for farming that prized casket of oil from blubber,
Whale worth its weight in gold, if wood, a vast source of lumber.

It is Boyd Tower of which we speak, a very fitting building,
Damaged by storm many years before, to eye, pleasant, appealing,
It offered a scene, from south to north, of strategic importance,
Allowing the Davidsons to launch boats first, a great assurance.

And where whale-sign was missed, obscured, nothing to assist,
If some dark cloak, shrouding mist, or did unexplainably desist,
There was the comfort in knowing that Tom would appear,
Flop-tailing to his heart's content, to lead on, to cleverly steer.

SONG OF THE OCEAN

When whale-sign of any description did speak out,
There was only one action to take amid shout,
Jim would find himself straddled upon his horse,
Racing home near Kiah, the beast beneath knowing the course.

Near approach of home he did raise the alarm,
Alerting all of the approaching whale, of which to harm,
To massacre and farm, to beach and snare, to harness and work,
This is how it played, not easy, not like taking baby from stork.

He sped on to raise the alarm of approaching foe,
The sound of the hooves most penetrating: hear it, you know,
The still of the night failing to masquerade,
Not mistaking the sound, this was no charade.

This was the still of the night,
A messenger to pass on great delight,
News which was to be acted upon, without a doubt,
Message received before Jim could dismount, men running about.

Three boats made the water and in good time,
To make their way across the smooth surface so sublime,
Water reflecting the star amidst clear skies high above,
Moving out towards the mouth of the bay they did all love.

And here we see that Jim may have misinterpreted a sign,
Nothing immediately seen, nothing on sight to align,
So an early morning patrol commenced from here,
To search for whale-sign, to all hope, hold it dear.

ORCINUS ORCA

They could only hope their efforts would be rewarded,
By quick find, quick catch, time on water not retarded,
Continuing to work the oars they moved ever on, into the night,
Towards the shelter at South Head, on occasion a delightful sight.

A large rock, reasonably easy to see by day, red in colour,
A wharf [so to speak] close to cave of occasional favour,
A cave here of substantial size and cover, a tether,
Great place to temporarily reside during inclement weather.

The crews deposited a few stores here,
An opportunity now to replenish, seldom did opportunity peer,
A place of rough comfort in time of great need,
Not a place to willingly submit, but get away from with speed.

They continued to stroke the ocean and moved out of the head,
And here they could see spouts from orca most easily read,
Coming up from Leather Jacket Bay,
The sun commencing its reveal, light transcending upon the grey.

The orca seemed relaxed and complacent,
Neither thrashing about, flop-tailing, or making a statement,
And further behind those up front,
Another spout of water, ready for the hunt.

The waterspout jettison from within,
The force pushing with it much water to air, to thin,
Misty vapours spouting about the ocean now calm, not wild,
Greeting the morning, so brilliant and mild.

SONG OF THE OCEAN

They were at work, listening intently,
Upon the sounds and movement of the ocean most discreetly,
Endeavouring to catch that ever elusive signal,
Of a whale within distance most reasonable.

The pods were positioned at varying intervals and in good fashion,
Three pods not far from coast, ears awaiting for that percussion,
Combined they acted as a barrier, a curtain,
Deciphering sounds and movement, soon to be, most certain.

And if a whale were to be moving too far out at ocean,
The killers would decide if whether or not to give compassion,
Or draw and force the whale towards the harpoon and lance,
For the men on green boats to have their chance.

It was a reality of the varied situations,
Of the killers' abilities and their reactions,
Whether or not the energy spent was worth the chase,
Each scenario must be measured from case to case.

Tom had seen the patrol of three boats and summed up the action,
Knew that the men were working with ocean, in conjunction,
Searching about and waiting for sign,
Hoping for a good sized baleen most fine.

Patrolling, waiting the opportunity to strike,
Hoping for chance not to sour, but situation to like,
Was it in fact a sign that Jim had seen,
From Boyd Tower, his eye so eager, so keen.

ORCINUS ORCA

Was it a dream, false hope delivered to eye,
Was it an error, misfortune he could not deny,
Was there something to occur real soon,
Was there to be hope in reflection of moon.

For the moon was rising,
Giving its gift, not surprising,
Not good for the baleen but aiding the men and orca alike,
Orcinus to encompass, employ their very bodies, to strike.

Tom now turned towards the others nice and slow,
Movement deliberate, before commencement of the show,
It was then that a signal was received,
From several miles out to ocean, clearly perceived.

A small whale was bypassing the mouth of Twofold Bay,
A minke whale with unborn calf, alone, a stray,
Though not enough to feed three, let alone a single pod,
Sufficient enough to aid in hunger and so given the nod.

The teeth of the upper jaw fit snugly into the lower,
Cogs of a steel wheel, with just as much power,
Their mouths closed but ready to rip and tear,
They now shifted into higher gear.

The killers' jaws opened and closed in quick succession,
Clapping their jaws together in mounting aggression,
To press the fear of the impending doom,
Deep within the minke's mind, a clear, unfortunate gloom.

SONG OF THE OCEAN

The signal was their call to duty,
A call to move forward, to gain on their booty,
Unbeknown to the men in the boats, orca beneath ocean face,
Mammals racing towards the ocean, with speed and much grace.

To the minke, to pester and provoke,
To embrace most diligently with restricting yoke,
By all means open to them, never to refrain,
No sympathy, just yield, a little sustenance to gain.

The minke would be fairly easy to catch,
No real competition, no equal match,
Hardly worth even this small effort,
Barely enough to provide any comfort.

But the facts of the case were mounted as normal,
No source of food shrugged off as dreary or abysmal,
And the mink would not tax them too harshly,
Quick and easy, over with briskly.

The normal procedure for the killers of Eden,
To undertake when hunting a minke, orca embolden,
See it stranded in the shallows, an easy win, never to fail,
And then consume it of all that was on offer, head to tail.

Although the same size as Orcinus, the leviathan of Eden town,
Was unable to outrun orca, being out of its class, to be run down,
In particular where a large pack of hungry mouths are concerned,
Looking for a quick fix, no time to waste, they cannot be spurned.

ORCINUS ORCA

The minke swam through the ocean, through wave, to slaughter,
The beak, pointed shape of his head, gliding through the water,
Twenty-nine feet in length and powering along at great speed,
But not quick enough to escape, not as fast, the desired need.

Flukes broad and concave along the notched rear,
Fins pointed at the tips, body streamlined, symmetry to steer,
It dove, arching tail stock high, flukes beneath much wave,
The commencement of a deep dive, attack to stave.

The minke was forced to surface, dive cut short,
Two killers calling an end to her effort, an effort to abort,
Subdued to further torment, no more days in life to chalk,
To tear chunks from her flank, no longer content to simply stalk.

All were so eager to feed, to finish, to kill her,
Not caring for the terror within which they stir,
The rush of red billowing out and merging with the ocean,
Large clouds expanding out, growing larger, an interaction.

Several sharks in the vicinity could hear the calling,
The dinner bell ringing, the Orcinus mauling,
but fear prevented them from approaching too close,
For even the Great White feared this gluttonous pose.

The minke was utterly surrounded,
May as well be immobile, grounded,
Bulge in stomach an unborn, undeniable,
Easily seen, unborn whale, fresh stock, reliable.

SONG OF THE OCEAN

The minke was not scrawny by any measure,
But not enough to satisfy three pods, no great treasure,
Preference, of course, was for a much larger baleen,
But there was none about, nothing heard, nothing seen.

Fresh dolphins, porpoises and fish,
Were always a welcomed dish,
But larger morsel was always their wish,
Small portion simply retarded... eish.

The minke was a krill feeder,
Harmless and often alone, easy fodder,
Life to end, to the wind seemingly thrown,
Unborn in womb, life to be never known.

The minke was eaten, of it all,
Nothing to hold the tide, nothing to stall,
Not an ounce of flesh or fat to remain,
Nothing but upon ocean a red stain.

And the men could only shrug off the situation,
Nothing for them to harvest, a purely sad position,
Normal patrol duty resumed, along with emotional stability,
Silence restored to the ocean, now strangled by tranquillity.

ORCINUS ORCA

THE UNFETTERED

George burst through the door and exclaimed for all to hear,
With such exhilarated enthusiasm that heads quickly did appear,
A message for the crews to man their particular boat,
Great excitement reverberating through his throat.

A great anxiousness fell over them all, so sheer, almost pain,
Heart throbs, pushing the coarse excitement through vein,
Excitement for that word, the word to greet at culmination,
Culmination of wit, to call 'RUSHO', that single congratulation.

Tom could be seen, flop-tailing in front of Kiah Inlet,
Sandbar spit separating it from the bay, already met,
The bar where the Lawrence Frost does rest,
Ghostly remains, a tombstone at its best.

So rapidly men threw themselves upon the thwarts, lacking grins,
Grabbing oars, thrusting them into water via the thole pins,
Safety jackets pushed aside and boots forced on by the few,
So little time to respond to the words that they loved, they knew.

The boats practically flew through the air of this bright day,
The afternoon air fresh with several clouds racing across the bay,
And all indication lead to it being a long night affair,
The sun more than likely to fall before killers, of meat, could tear.

SONG OF THE OCEAN

Quick kill is required, now more than ever, the need to be clever,
If whale was not secured by nightfall the air would cause fever,
Blasted cold, hindrance worse than a storm, a wind-chill factor,
A chill so devilishly severe: could shave a man of calm like razor.

Tom, having seen the rush of men to boats in good essence,
Was assured by their fast action, soon to be in his presence,
Turned tail, his flukes thrashing at the surface with grace,
Gaining a little depth below the surface in good pace.

Tom soon picked up on the signals of pods and right whale,
Signals through water clear as a bell, ripe and not stale,
And he was still some distance from the fight as it was heard,
Thrashing of flippers and flukes, amidst calm ocean, deciphered.

Echolocation engulfed the area, ocean a conductor, better than air,
Penetrating all, and in any direction you cared to stare,
The picture being painted in strong transcendent, bright colour,
Echolocation, a sensitive sensory system, chords of many flavour.

It was ten times more accurate than the best sonar in submarines,
Echoes, short pulses of sound, not indicative of machines,
Pulses; echoes emitted via staccato styles, high-frequency sound,
Each lasting a few milliseconds, but some longer can be found.

Produced in the nasal passage and deeper,
Below the blow hole, each the keeper,
Directed to the front, passing through fatty tissue of forehead,
Which in turn acted as a lens, musical vocabulary, easily read.

ORCINUS ORCA

He endeavoured to focus his sound, for it to be well directed,
Hearing and advising, all taken for granted,
Segments of the emitted sound refracted, clearly understood,
Sound returning through bony walls of lower jaw, as it would.

There is so, so much here,
So much to clarify, to appear,
Such as sound being transmitted along the jaws length,
To acoustic conduits, magnificent evolution amidst such strength.

From conduits to sensory organs, their middle ear, sound to gain,
One on either side of the skull near the base of the brain,
This was an ultrasound in effect a clear picture, a distinct function,
Pictures painted clear, scene formed, acted upon, instant reaction.

The returning sound, travelling at four times greater speed,
Than that through the air, as fast as they require and need,
Providing detailed analyses, much information of varied texture,
Size, shape, distance, and composition, all as one, or as mixture.

Tom concentrated upon the object of his desire,
To bombard it further, information to acquire,
To be precise, to expose clear weakness,
For attack and closure to be one of neatness.

And the three boats of Davidson's men had much style,
Pulled in unison at first, slightly askew but all in file,
Each beckoned by their headsman to be the first in range,
For harpoon and lance to be thrown, a kill to arrange.

SONG OF THE OCEAN

Colourful language was filling the air,
But these were hard men, hard but fair,
Voices carried haphazardly, far and wide across the bay,
Observers from the banks hearing each word as it stray.

But those watching paid little heed to each, foul, uttered word,
Men spurring each other on, words employed instead of sword,
For this was just a part of the play, it was all part and parcel,
Water off a duck's back, for this was a battle in which to marvel.

And the voiced encouragement continued, not seeming to abate,
Compared to the symphony of choruses below, how did it relate?
Were the killers speaking of same tone,
Of this it will never be known.

Then appeared one of their competitors, it was like a grievance,
Oars striking the water with as much unrestrained jubilance,
A competitor having launched two boats, how deplorable,
But all was fair in love and war, nevertheless, feelings ropable.

Spray lifted from the bows as muscles taut,
Pressing for a little extra speed, gain that naut,
surmounting efforts of gigantean proportion,
Stress reflected on all faces, a contortion.

Their teeth were exposed to the world,
Grimaces painted on faces, their minds twirled,
Deep lines of controlled aggression,
Upon their faces was bore great expression.

ORCINUS ORCA

This was a race for survival, for the promise of wages,
For promise of purse, the writing of historical pages,
For a little coin, for the security of their families,
For the appeasement of all, and all part of the formalities.

Each and every one that manned an oar put in a great effort,
Dwarfed all else, the headsman's no less, great lack of comfort,
Each and every man full of character, measured by agility,
Performing each task, controlling sweeps, all with great ability.

Maintaining good direction,
To hone and deliver that perfection,
Enormous amounts of instilled confidence,
Encouragement pouring from all pores, the way of deliverance.

This was all for the sake of 'fast fish',
Nothing else mattered but this, their true wish,
But was this a fair fight, with the pods on Davidson's side,
Could this be condoned, as upon gentle waves they ride.

The total number of killers unknown, with three pods further out,
A second whale further still, bypassing: to strike, to clout,
Regardless, the tactics for the hunt did remain the same,
No variation from usual procedure: this was survival, not a game.

Tom turned then, instinctively, a sprint from starting gate,
Hearing the oars on water, time for whale to meet his fate,
Time to begin the wrestle, time for torment and achievement,
Time to dig that grave, a cup of victory, to brim with contentment.

SONG OF THE OCEAN

The right whale was slow, turned towards the mouth of the bay,
Towards the boats that drew nearer, minds of men clear as day,
Each passing second bringing terror and death all the closer,
Boats continuing to surge forward, neither wishing to be the loser.

The gap between all parties now closed at a tremendous rate,
Each drawn as though a magnet to the whale, the beast, the bait,
And then the right sounded, diving beneath the ocean ceiling,
Sending all into turmoil, feelings reeling.

But this was just a temporary stay,
For the killers acted fast, not allowing it to stray,
The leviathan forced to surface and remain in sight,
For harpooner to try for that hard and fast, steel bite.

A harpooner's kiss,
If it did not miss,
The securing of whale to boat,
Fingers around a man's throat.

And the whale dove again but for only a short time,
Again to surface but so hazardous, a coin spinning on dime,
For Whelan, the contender, had a boat where it did surface,
Uplift of whale and water seeing a Whelan boat slow its pace.

No pace to attain, none to pursue, uplifted by strength and might,
For they were momentarily assailed, upon the back of the right,
Not just a look of surprise, but also shock and terror,
Fell upon the faces of Whelan's men together.

ORCINUS ORCA

Now riding for brief moment upon the back of this hulk,
Held high aloft upon the crest of their passions bulk,
The seal between water and air broke,
Oars no longer in the ocean, unable to stroke.

Oars magically lifted from the water,
Still full of fight this great monster,
And the men aboard considered jumping from their boat,
Each no longer having wish, nor heart, to gloat.

Jump from this peril and into another,
Frying pan to fire, flames you cannot smother,
But suddenly and with great relief, sanity returning,
The boat slid harmlessly back to water, slightly turning.

Tom took an instinctive second to peruse the situation above,
To spy upon surface, attain position of those he seemed to love,
The green boats of Davidson seen close to Whelan's: too close,
This was reality, close call, a conflagration, too large in dose.

He could see, of Davidson's boat, the harpooner stand ready,
Weapon of trade upon his shoulder, surprisingly quite steady,
Thigh braced against the thwart and ready with strength to fling,
With great accuracy his iron, to kiss, to secure 'fast fish', to sting.

It left his hand then and fell towards the right whale,
Insufficient power behind the throw, and now for short tale,
For the harpooner was called Pigeon, employed for his skill,
But the wages from Davidson's could not meet the bill.

SONG OF THE OCEAN

For over time evidence had been accumulated,
Pigeon's skill had been assessed and well rated,
The harpooner was cowardly being employed by Whelan,
Drawn by promise of payment and wage, good word and reason.

And so the throw was set to task with lack in power,
To provide assistance, upon Whelan, this fortune a shower,
A shower of blessings, to steal from Davidson and the Orca,
For Whelan to keep for himself, to be the deliverer of slaughter.

It was the last throw that Pigeon would, for Davidson, ever make,
There was simply too much here at stake,
The loss of the whale meant his immediate termination,
Paid off by Whelan, Pigeon's loyalty found at another station.

But the task at hand was still rather hazardous from all the boat,
Whale harried by the killers, restrained as though by moat,
And then suddenly the jaw of John Davidon did drop in disbelief,
From a man in Whelan's second boat, Bedford, a shout most brief.

Bedford had tossed his harpoon most expertly,
Secured victory most assuredly,
Energy, precision, a testament to his ability,
The 'fast fish' tied up, a situation of gravity.

Why gravity?
Lack of amity,
Read further,
An Orca tether.

ORCINUS ORCA

Whelan began with his lancing,
Unable to stop his periodic glancing,
Looking upon the green boats with smirk on face,
For the Davidsons and orca alike, a sheer disgrace.

The harpoon, yes, did stick fast,
Did not fall, it was there to last,
For the whale there was no escaping the trap,
For it, there would be only that eternal nap.

Regardless, however, of the dire situation,
The right performed a gigantean persuasion,
It sprang to entrance of the bay, an attempt made for open water,
To embrace the wide-open space, be free of harpoon, of slaughter.

Pulling the boat, the men along for the short ride,
Upon the surface it did seemingly glide,
Endeavouring to escape the manila rope,
To try and achieve escape, to regain that lost hope.

John saw the dilemma and fell upon the only conclusion,
The battle had been lost due to an obscured conviction,
The unsteady hand, slow reaction time, of one of his own,
Pigeon, soon to be a figure on the unemployment line in town.

Davidson and crew could not believe what their eyes reflected,
The right whale giving up its fight for life, sooner than expected,
Pelted well by the two boats that were in good position,
One on either side, throwing lance after lance without question.

SONG OF THE OCEAN

If not for the help provided by the killers, upon huge beast,
Then the kill would have been enduring, to say the least,
And now, in the cold victory that had been won, without stop,
Whelan was towing the carcass in towards his workshop.

Close enough to tow, no need to sink and await the bloat,
Just tow the dead whale in by power of oar, by power of boat,
And as they tugged on their oars the killers came for their reward,
To sup on lips and tongue, their just gift, the one men could afford.

Whelan's men would have none of this, no agreement bestowed,
Picked up tools-of-the-trade, tools on board having been stowed,
Their spades, square in shape and very sharp, very sharp indeed,
Those used in deblubbering, now served another desire and need.

They were striking at the killers, shear lack of remorse,
Keeping them at bay, provoking reaction, being coarse,
Holding back their attempts to take what was theirs,
Denying them food to survive amidst silent but snarly glares.

Tom surfaced and looked the men in the eyes,
Upon each and every one, for they, he did despise,
He took note of the boats, to remember them well,
Of this great rudeness, to the others he would tell.

Davidson's boats were green,
To help them the Orcinus were keen,
Combined effort to reward both in equal measure,
But Whelan: never again would he receive his treasure.

ORCINUS ORCA

To always be remembered, never forgotten,
To the core they were very rotten,
Never again to be provided opportunity,
Endeavour to always obscure their ability.

No longer would they provide,
Unequivocal assistance, an easy ride,
Not as much as a wink,
No recognition, not even a blink.

SONG OF THE OCEAN

THE FIGHT

The sun had not even commenced to light the day,
When two of the killers came flop-tailing upon the bay,
Throwing themselves out of ocean, to crash upon rolling wave,
The wind shallow but so cold, which hard work could stave.

Weather was an important factor within this industry learned,
In particular where the crews were concerned,
A hard south-west wind was cold,
The effect seeing the ocean become rather bold.

Choppy in the concave and here to stay,
Within reach and up to the mouth of Twofold bay,
For further out to ocean the waves did swell,
Though not enough to ring an alarm bell.

Rough by the layman's point of view,
The normalcy would not know what to do,
Hands of sweet work, not rough,
Would find it too arduous and extremely tough.

Swells could become worse,
Ever searching for that rancid curse,
Or settle,
To be gentle.

ORCINUS ORCA

But for that present it was not that strange,
Within tolerances, within that range,
For the present, however, all was fair,
RUSHO so shouted, to boats from lair.

The chase to commence, blubber soon to be won,
George 14, full of vigour, extremely keen, finding it fun,
As all others, their jackets were thrown upon their bulk,
George was ready, well stoked, to work hard, never to skulk.

Scrambling out from the bunkhouse door,
Time of day and tiredness they were to ignore,
Running as fast as legs could carry them to their work,
Like greyhounds unleashed from pen, to whale which lurk.

The whale had entered the bay,
In search of fish, to do as he may,
To steal the solace, to enjoy his stay,
All alone and easy pickings, easy prey.

Suddenly it could be heard there in the night,
Some men slightly astounded: no, no, not feeling fright,
Excitement it was they felt within,
It was a whale, no false alarm, faces lighting up with broad grin.

Somewhere just inside the mouth of the bay, no longer at frolic,
Where many killers were present, organising tactics with logic,
To attempt to coral this beast with all their might,
To keep the whale from heading out to ocean this night.

SONG OF THE OCEAN

It was a humpback, not in a good position,
Though plump and blubberous, in good condition,
Forced to remain within the confines of bay,
Between rock and hard place, how gloomy, how grey.

The killers could taste the tongue as they did move,
Reared and ready, in mood for killing, in the groove,
Adversely the headsman was considering his reward,
The tonnage of oil to be obtained, for he the steward.

The men wasted no time at all in closing the gap,
Between themselves and the fray, battling, no time for nap,
Muscles to be cleaved and hacked as they powered along,
Burning and working, men build hard, hard and strong.

Now fully awake and aware of their senses,
A straight and seemingly easy road to prize, no fences,
Knowing full well that the killers would be there,
You could not currently see them, but they were doing their share.

The lights from the bunkhouse and cottage now far behind,
Gradually growing smaller and smaller, comfort now out of mind,
No light of moon to aid them, the sky filled with cloud this night,
Only hard and strenuous work stifled the cold of its bite.

Somewhere upon this earth the sun was shining bright,
The crust of the earth feeling comfort so tight,
Elsewhere the sky was clear and stars sparkled above so high,
But here, right now, there was nothing, no slice of pie.

ORCINUS ORCA

But something to appease, something here for layman to learn,
For all bay whalers know of one thing to which you could turn,
When stalking whale by night, there happened a small reaction,
The clear presence, phosphorescent trails, tracks upon the ocean.

George sat upon the front, the forward most thwart,
Providing direction, employing this natural aid as taught,
Trails left by the killers were seemingly easy to follow,
For whale, these pursuers, it was strange, hard to swallow.

But progress was still slow,
In this Tom did feel, did know,
So he moves back alongside the leading boat,
If human you would say he was there to gloat.

Tom felt that the men were not working to task,
Wished more from them now, but unable to ask,
Was something amiss? These men, so inadequate,
Time was of the essence, time most desperate.

Tom pushed against the lead boat, shoving it aside,
Endeavouring to point out, he could aid the boat, give it a ride,
If only they were to think on the situation,
Understood his clear thinking, his ideas, his passion.

If a harpoon had been thrown then there would be a rope,
A rope could be pulled by Tom to aid the boat, give it hope,
In gaining speed and much time, to close the gap,
To reel in the humpback, from abstract and grey, to sound in lap.

SONG OF THE OCEAN

With the absence of the rope there was little Tom could do,
If only there was a way, if only the men knew,
But wrestling with the progress of the boat was doing little,
To invoke the imagination of those rowing was a battle.

Tom gave up, took off towards the humpback,
A few curses from the men beginning to stack,
Voices that momentarily bellowed out for miles and miles around,
Voices not mellow, picked up by the wind and carried to ground.

A wind was starting to pick up, to grow in its ferocity,
The cold night air now stinging at faces, a great sobriety,
Spray from ocean top,
Such weather you could not stop.

Coming up from the rolling waves, upon the bow so thrown,
Poor conditions commenced to make themselves known,
To the rowers of each boat doing duty, no spare oar to stow,
Each and every one feeling the chill commencing to grow.

As muscles tore,
At stroking of oar,
At battling each wave,
Great effort each man gave.

The headsman ordered for silence right then and there,
For the last thing he wished was to be forced to share,
If any competitor was to hear them chasing down a whale,
This very day's hunt and energy would be for nought and fail.

ORCINUS ORCA

They had lost one the day before, another would not do justice,
Heading now past Snug Cover, Eden, no need to provide notice,
Where sleeping inhabitants of town were, just that, sound asleep,
So few lanterns ablaze from early risers, to work so few did leap.

Tom and two others, moving just below the surface, clearly seen,
Bulges of ocean moving with them, evoked and keen,
Tops of their backs and a little fluke worthy of glance,
It was clear they were ready, despite lack of readable stance.

An old friend then decided to pay them a visit,
The most temporary appearance of the moon a credit,
Provided them the opportunity to clearly see the humpback's tail,
They were beginning to pester: to pester the whale to great avail.

The night was dark and spy-hopping was no guarantee,
Of good visual with either the men's boats or whale to see,
A visual glance of blowing and sucking in more air for dive,
For humpback to attempt an escape, to live and thrive.

The killers then decided on another action to take,
To force the whale deeper, deprive it of breathing, life at stake,
To see it use its air once and for all, sustenance depleted,
To deplete it emphatically of its facility, to drown, death greeted.

These were the thoughts that ran through Tom's mind,
The tactic they should employ, depriving men of their find,
Gone the men's ability to anchor the carcass,
Not to be part of a play, as per Whelan's raucous.

SONG OF THE OCEAN

But these were mammals of a society, of the oceans and seas,
Not men of selfish behaviours, of their steadfast pleas,
If the weather failed to improve and got any worse,
The carcass could drift out to ocean, most real, quite terse.

But Tom knew they needed man's power, to avoid a lengthy mess,
Needed the strength of harpoon and lance in order to relieve stress,
To siphon the humpback of will to live, increase the opportunity,
A kill by any means, no need to put men through great scrutiny.

And great achievement was received, the whale held tight,
Forced to enter further into the bay, lacking in thought, no flight,
Constantly parried by killers, remorseless strides of conviction,
Heighten the dilemma of humpback's predicament and restriction.

To savour the moment when they would gain the upper hand,
That mouthful of lip and tongue, the delicacy that was so grand,
But a sudden flex came, an ability to perform manoeuvres well,
The humpback shifted gear, gone the temperance, signs to tell.

It was now adamant to avoid the snapping of jaw,
Avoid the Orcinus as they lurched, reinforcing their law,
A great Chunk of blubber torn from his bulk,
These orca were not an animal used to shy action, to sulk.

The whale raced for the surface and broke it fast,
Great volumes of spray pelted here and there over area vast,
The rowers of a nearby boat smothered from head to foot in spray,
Shocking reality, a hellish dampening of feverish cold to stay.

ORCINUS ORCA

The cold of the ocean penetrating fast to the bone,
Stinging at their flesh, stupor over them thrown,
Numbing all feeling in their hands, face and toe,
Feelings that were the most horrific one ever comes to know.

But quality of will is a bequest any bay whaler had instilled,
Men of heart, confident of mind, their very cores filled,
And so they put aside this drenching of life-sucking cold,
Remained steadfast in conviction, of sound mind, calm and bold.

George saw the opportunity provided him and lifted the harpoon,
High and steady above his head in both hands and not too soon,
He thrust down hard at just the right time, power and transition,
Phosphorus sign and movement pointed to whale's position.

The point of the harpoon penetrated deep, well secure,
Secure and strong within the beast most sure,
The 'fast fish' had been secured, no time in victory to bask,
And Alex Greig's boat was called to inaction, pulled from task.

The last thing they wanted was for two harpoons to be stuck fast,
Two harpoons in one fish would ensure safety was not to last,
In particular at night when the weather was not sound,
Where much difficulty there was, in controlling boats, to be found.

Fred Wilson moved to the rear and changed seating,
Placed immediately with the headsman, formality, no greeting,
John's own boat conducted the same manoeuvre,
George moving to the rear and changing places with his father.

SONG OF THE OCEAN

The lancing of the whale was to commence immediately,
To secure good lance, not rash, but bold, not neatly,
The whale had reared its barnacled head at the initial stinging,
First harpoon and then lance, terror inwardly ringing.

The reality of the situation commenced to become clear,
A humpback of little threat to anyone or anything near,
Other than what was taken in his mouth and digested within,
Chased beneath and above the waves, having committed no sin.

He was meek and powerfully strong,
Meant no harm, did no wrong,
Wished only to move towards a breeding ground,
For mate to be secured, to be found.

To find himself a mate for the season of joy,
To secured and find, not to harass and destroy,
To pass on his genes at social gathering as per his peers,
To unknowingly secure the species for future years.

He sounded almost immediately on feeling the sting,
The harpoon entering his body, song for the thrower to sing,
And he dove as deep as he possibly could,
Manila rope dragging behind him as it would.

The rope looped around the loggerhead for control and ease,
Control which would not come easily upon worsening seas,
And whether Pacific Ocean or Tasman Sea,
Water was water, and to seamen no real discrepancy.

ORCINUS ORCA

With the killers aid, a strong pillar,
The men had less concern for failure,
Though some things can be unexpected,
Occurrences which should never be repeated.

But today was a relief,
Nothing outlandish to issue grief,
A reasonable night upon the wave,
Reasonable work, to manhood pave.

Nevertheless,
The whale felt stress,
With such he became unsteady,
For a lance he was not ready.

The temperament of a harpooned whale was unpredictable,
Easily pressed into thrashing about in a manner unstable,
A harpooned whale is a dangerous animal, through and through,
As dangerous as they come, flukes capable of cutting boat in two.

The ploy of the killers had now changed,
They saw with clarity, and heard, the boats now ranged,
Lances could be thrown and landed with hopeful effect,
For the harpoon sat fast, firm and erect.

The call went around for the pod to change tactic,
No need to further press humpback deeper, keep it basic,
Avoid loss of energy, keep firm and strong,
Make all the correct decisions and none of the wrong.

SONG OF THE OCEAN

Tom then leapt from the water,
His entire body lifting amidst the slow slaughter,
Coming down hard on back of humpback as though beckoned,
Sliding upon blowhole, restricting breathing, just for a second.

So impede that right, for the whale to breath, no reprieve,
To shorten his life, for it to vanish, to leave,
Remove his ability to think straight,
No longer able to act with precision first rate.

Tired to the core, from base,
Tired of the chase,
Tired of the restrictions imposed, a cloak of terror to wear,
Tired from the stress, strain, and overpowering fear

The whale was being forced to remain upon surface,
Killers either side and one below, their temperaments a furnace,
The boats closing in, drawing manila line through loggerhead,
Bringing the catch home, thread by thread.

George gave the order to turn towards the whale,
Picked up a lance before vision of monstrous tail,
He readied himself, thigh against thwart,
Steadying himself for whales fury, drowned in thought.

The gap was closed between them both,
He hurled the lance, his task to doth,
With great precision into the flank of the beast,
Between the ribs, soon upon the orca to feast.

ORCINUS ORCA

It penetrated deep and the whale curled in pain,
His head lifting out of the water for air to gain,
Spray covering the crew once more,
What other effects were there in store.

Particles of moisture drifted quickly away,
Droplets upon clothing, to the wind, its prey,
The rough and churning, the rolling of wave,
White crests forming, breaking, not to behave.

The humpback endeavoured to sound one more time: or his last,
Flukes lifting out of the water, so near, so hugely vast,
Alex Greig's boat coming close to being badly hammered,
Crashing of tail unsettling those on board as they stammered.

A warning broke the air for all oars to be peaked,
To ready themselves for a fate, blood soaked and streaked,
Preparing themselves to be delivered into the waters around,
Amidst fury of whale and Orcinus, unsavoury death to be found.

For no one knew if the killers held a taste for human flesh,
Whether man-flesh, within their teeth, did ever mesh,
None found comfort in this thought by any distinct measure,
None wished to find out, if this was to be an orca pleasure.

The tremendous crash came quick and loud,
Failed to hit anything brittle, but much water displaced, a shroud,
A prayer said by many, to have escaped a watery tomb,
Boat not to capsize with men: nor oars of blade, handle and loom.

SONG OF THE OCEAN

So the battle continued to be waged, a further two, sturdy lance,
Thrown at first chance, very next clear shot, clear glance,
Breaching the shell of the humpback and the 'red flag' flew,
A piercing, deafening noise erupted then, and everyone knew.

When finally the victory was achieved, most solidly won,
The carcass afloat, being mauled by the killers, mother and son,
Whale's mouth forced open, tongue and lips taken from beast,
The crews sat back exhausted, watched as the killers did feast.

It was now that George gave the order,
Certainly no time to saunter,
For a lantern to be lit, the beginning of their transition,
Each boat did comply, to aid them in their ambition.

A little light in order to acquire their desire and need,
For tomorrow, blubber! to appease their hunger, their greed,
The light was but to assist, attaching an anchor to whale, the toll,
And for positions in boats to be changed with ease and control.

The job was done, the fight lasting fifty minutes, no more,
And some to secure anchor, a task upon which for energy to pour,
No sooner had they finished and the sun made its appearance,
Right then and there it did show: goodbye to night, the hindrance.

All eyes then fell upon the biggest humpback seen in the bay,
Either dead or alive its size hard to fathom, not abstract or grey,
It was 52 feet long and quite literally dwarfed all before,
So hard it was to think of but a memory for all time and more.

ORCINUS ORCA

Yes indeed, one to recall when drunk, to be stammered,
This day amongst many others would be remembered,
Another story to fill the ears of drinkers at public house,
But no real story here to share with lover or spouse.

This was a turning point that moulded George's life forever,
Sculpting his youth, to be part of him, a constant tether,
For he to follow in the footsteps of his father before,
From these his early years, to worship work, the orca, their law.

The glamorous side of things he would see to come and go,
Beginning with this short adventure: of all to come and know,
Men and orca working as one, to turn the tide of bay whaling,
Upon the head, to hammer, to fasten hope, to secure by nailing.

And this site of the slaying was visited once again,
Twenty-four hours after ending the humpbacks life in pain,
Orcinus having drawn their meal to watery depths to feed,
A temporary place of rest before rising, men to harvest their need.

The carcass had filled with gas,
Until it floated to the surface, a great mass,
Floating upon gentle wave, looking a real mess,
But now they must tow it, a relief, no stress.

It was hard work but stress free and rewarding,
Unless shark did appear, a prize for gorging,
Floating upright, its back bare for the world to see,
Underbelly obscured beneath the waves, floating free.

SONG OF THE OCEAN

The anchor retrieved, rower's arms bent to the labour, to deliver,
Deliver the whale, being turned in over near the Towamba River,
Bringing home the prize, to try-works for deblubbering,
Where capstan and boiling pots sat ready and waiting.

Boat spades were picked up by the men that had gathered,
Sharpened points, sharp as could possibly be, shapes not tapered,
The blubber cut into squares with great effort and much sweat,
Wiping salt of flesh from brow, shirt sleeves soaked, no regret.

Seagulls filled the air, brought together by that silent ringing,
Sound of dinner bell, to congregate amidst squawking, not singing,
Swooping in and pestering the work detail to no avail,
Making a right nuisance of themselves without fail.

The stench about was wretched, beyond belief,
From it there was little to no relief,
For the seagulls the perfume of any God,
To their approval they would give the nod.

The entire process was hard and extremely laborious,
Sheets of blubber cut from the whale in manner most serious,
Then turned up the ramp, further work undertaken on the blubber,
Each large portion being cut into strips: and not at leisure.

Strips that were 15 inches x 5 inches x 5 inches deep,
Deep as the blubber, as deep of that which they were to reap,
Strips then cast into a large vat to be minced smaller,
Portions placed within try-pots there on this spot, the boiler.

ORCINUS ORCA

A man then has the duty to skim the surface,
Skim with a perforated utensil, for the smell a grimace,
Watching, attending, the boiling take place,
This was their source of wage, to render there was no race.

Some tasked with ensuring that all went well of their toil,
That all was rendered sufficiently, a pure, pure oil,
Pouring this into smaller pots, later into numerous casket,
Ready for shipping, for sale, ready for market.

SONG OF THE OCEAN

THE POD

It was 1890, a sad time for all,
Three short years, time to fall,
Typee and Humpy to leave here today,
Mayhap to return, mayhap to stay away.

Never a crystal ball affair,
Nothing firm in which to stare,
The two orca spoken were birds of a feather,
Stuck hard and firm, always together.

To leave behind friends was always a sad time for all,
But there was never any hard fact, any hard rule,
If one felt a need to leave, to adventure elsewhere, to depart,
Then that should be permitted, to recommence, to restart.

A sad parting, in particular with Stranger, their living power,
More than matriarch, more than strength during times gone sour,
But the breeding season had come around,
Excitement to seek out, adventure to be found.

Breeding season: some would leave, some would show,
No way to be sure, no way to know,
But for the majority the pods remained the same,
But still, it was a terrible shame.

ORCINUS ORCA

Perhaps Orcinus has different feelings than human mothers,
Different views and understandings unknown to others,
The love Stranger felt would be rekindled by the mean,
By the basic principles and balance of all that could be seen.

As averages go this could be considered a good turn,
Most had experienced similar, of it to learn,
But orca like Tom were here to stay,
Never to turn tail, never to stray.

For the whalers of the bay, the keen eye saw,
Changing each year the saddle patches thaw,
Then the new sprout to blossom and grow,
For each to be named, for each to befriend and to know.

Typee would be missed for his exuberance, his will to win,
Humpy for her ability to lead attacks, ripping blubber with grin,
Her dorsal, of all the other, a flag upon her back, forever,
Bent completely over, easily spotted from distance, fast learner.

The pod gathered around the couple at a place slightly north,
Not far from the icy coast of the South Pole for what it is worth,
Resting as they did between attacks on seals, oblivious they stray,
Taking opportunity for rest and before returning to Twofold Bay.

Typee and Humpy looked upon the members of their fraternity,
Their brothers and sisters like kin, their clan, their identity,
They stared a deep and longing stare, a submissive look,
Farewelling, feeling sad, sorrow, time together, pages from book.

SONG OF THE OCEAN

But why leave now,
To seemingly throw in the towel,
It was to explore new environments, rear young, learn tactics,
To learn new routines, new feeding techniques, new 'basics'.

Typee was set upon starting afresh, strong in conviction,
Sling the reigns away and to live with no restriction,
And so with the goodbyes given the pair of killers turned tail,
Swam from those they knew well, to be relied upon without fail.

And time passed as it does, the older we are, the faster time falls,
Seconds, minutes, hours and years, never slows, never stalls,
It had been some time now that Typee and Humpy had departed,
When the appearance of another turned heads, hearts started.

Stranger was the first to approach the killer whale,
A strong resemblance to Typee, no significance to fail,
But despite similarities there was no relation,
Jackson was not a by-product of Typee and Humpy attraction.

At first glance,
Their very stance,
Their saddle patch,
All did seemingly match.

The pod gathered to introduce themselves, new member found,
A little vocalisation, skin rubbing and general nosing around,
Jackson, now member of the team, accepting his position,
Happy to fit in, happy to receive that 'new member' recognition.

ORCINUS ORCA

It wasn't known from where he did feed,
Not overly thin, able to tend own need,
He was a stray from somewhere, of this all were sure,
Of no real importance, not yet, but one not prone to be immure.

Possibly discarded by another matriarch for disobedient behaviour,
Likely a transient looking for change, just another harbour,
A harbour that might offer him better opportunity in the future,
He, a new mind upon which to feed, did appear most mature.

He may even have lost a loved one and felt a strong urge to leave,
Depart the pod of which he was a member, start afresh, not grieve,
Regardless of circumstance, haply so fast, bonds to grow strong,
From outward appearance, all mused, he could not go wrong.

Jackson, a male of eleven years, average length from head to tail,
Saw immediate wonder and appeal in one of the younger female,
She was Sharkey and much time together they did share,
Each years from sexual maturity, friendship lacking in fanfare.

At first the attraction wasn't sexual or inappropriate,
Over no ruling did he stray, of bounds did not deviate,
Sharkey had appearance of one he previously knew,
A kindling of flame, of hard-felt love, a love which grew.

They were considered, through due cause, a pair,
To couple one day, all so pleasant and fair,
A time so great, to work together, always keen,
Vapours of mist upon dark horizon not yet seen.

SONG OF THE OCEAN

THE PROTECTION

George lances his first humpback, a small animal by measure,
Providing confidence in these early years, and ample pleasure,
Not much pleasure for the whale so pierced, coming off worse,
The new headsman, seen as aspiring young man, seemingly terse.

Aspiration forming like the callous upon a working man's hand,
Great victory short lived, toast of company, man of the band,
But the kill was followed by many weeks of frustration,
No kill to be procured, no oil the render, nought to fashion.

George and his crew, along with John and his own,
Sheltered at South Head, wharf of rock, together, never alone,
Settled within the cave of substantial size,
Awaiting the call to action, that eluding prize.

The weather was fine and easier to put out boats from the cave,
Call for rapid response heard, for further misfortune to be stave,
Beneath the helm, South Head, at the ready, eagerness to grow,
Providing ability to move fast when whale decided to show.

The men had polished off lunch, now at rest with mugs of tea,
Tantalizing their senses when a sudden call came, a cry, a plea,
From atop the cliff and approaching fast, whale had been sighted,
Followed closely by six killers, the men were so delighted.

ORCINUS ORCA

It was a right whale of large… no; massive proportions,
Filled with desire to mate and feed, of many notions,
And so far off it was hard to decipher, as killers did lure,
But two of the dorsal were those of Tom and Hooky for sure.

By the time the two boats were cast from the rocky wharf,
The whale, which killers and men in boats could never dwarf,
Had been pressured into the mouth of Twofold Bay,
In an attempt to harass, to kill, to feed upon as killers may.

Tom and Hooky separated from the mustering, with aching teeth,
Remainder of pod streamlining along on all sides and beneath,
The two keeping the front clear, paving the way, demise to cast,
Like the script of a movie, to fulfil each scene to the very last.

Tom and Hooky swam about the boats, instilling hope,
Just for short period, men preparing harpoon, lance and rope,
Each and all accessing the situation for what it was worth,
John's boat pulling away from George's, to go ever forth.

Kind and straight forward insults were pressed upon the crews,
Curse from headsman to headsman, encouragement, old news,
Verbal assaults of friendly gestures and coercion,
Aptitude, self confidence, in a word, inspiration.

Each man took control of his own ambition,
Here there was no hunger, no malnutrition,
Oars employed to their fullest, with great control they pull,
Potential of the crews, and individuals, never a lull.

SONG OF THE OCEAN

And in time potential indeed did peak,
It comes to reason, no need of this to truly speak,
For great effort can only go so far with no rest,
To perform to the extreme, to one's absolute best.

The culmination of effort saw the boats approach their target,
All wishing within to win the day, get oil to market,
Tom and Hooky seeing the men making ground, faring well,
Departed the boats, to re-join their pod, amidst the growing swell.

The whale was heading for John's boat, John ready to stand,
Ready the harpooner, take position, get that iron firmly in hand,
The harpooner scrambled to position, bracing against the thwart,
Eyeing the whale with suspicion, preparing strike as self taught.

George acted upon the situation, moved to the starboard,
Shifting position and approach, to pursue that target and reward,
Wondering whether it may surface from beneath his father's boat,
Seeing it happen, right now, yoke temporarily fall from throat.

For Alex let loose with power, the muscle, of memory, it knew,
Harpoon racing through the air to target, slightly off skew,
The moving target too far, the shot did not penetrate,
Striking just below the dorsal, a poor throw, too poor to rate.

The fish was considered fast but that is too bold,
A whale this size could easily escape the hold,
Quite readily release himself of this embrace,
To continue on with this ultimate, survival race.

ORCINUS ORCA

Sam Haddigaddi obeyed the order, prepared to sling another,
Another harpoon, but this like clap of thunder,
Peering momentarily at Alex, a friendly suggestion, competitive,
Harpoon steady in hand, gaining calculation, gaining perspective.

He savoured this moment, his take on the right whale,
To see if he could do better, where Alex did fail,
Commiserations for the one that did not achieve,
Achieve that fast fish, congratulations Alex would not receive.

Now, a throw which he had made many times in the past,
One which people would speak of, a victory to last,
One which would make him a legend of the bay,
An asset for the Davidson's, for ever and a day.

He hurled it then as the monster passed them by, not to be denied,
Hounded by the killers as they took chunks from each side,
Another orca beyond and one much further down,
The containment holding firm, the whale unable to leave town.

And as the harpoon was hurled towards the right whale,
The oars were dug into the ocean, ignoring any need to pail,
Quickly reverse, shift approach of the boat: go: halt,
Dig in deep to the ocean, see that whale trying to bolt.

Boat and whale just missed,
All fear now dismissed,
No collision, lucky in that, at least,
Avoiding ride upon back of beast.

SONG OF THE OCEAN

The line was secure and the loggerhead attended,
Water now pailed out, poured over line, situation amended,
For the loggerhead was becoming too hot, smouldering,
Always vigilant, watchful eye the nurse, avoid floundering.

The headsman was changing places with the harpooner,
Commanded and completed, far better is to be all the sooner,
Two ropes now connected to the whale, beneath dorsal,
Two boats now in tow, oil in sight, for orca a great morsel.

John was closer to the whale than George, perchance,
George several boat lengths behind, further to throw each lance,
Both towed upon the waves, upon open ocean, quite unsheltered,
Killers trying to muster, the largest whale they had encountered.

The whale, having had enough,
Being large and very tough,
Tried heading out to ocean, open water,
Boats in tow, for killers no saunter.

Orcinus, their constant barrage, their preventing,
Not allowing the whale to dive, unrelenting,
At sides, beneath, snapping at heels, or so the speak,
Biting at flanks, covering blowhole, any favourable tweak.

But the whale kept on going, refused to say nay,
Heading further and further from neck of bay,
Out towards the east, the sun having deserted, to rest,
Last fragrant of light passing over range to the west.

ORCINUS ORCA

To the west, where their home beckoned for the men to return,
Where warmth of fire and hot food sat ready for stomach to churn,
Alas, not much for it, but to sit back and wait for the whale to tire,
For boats in tow to finish with lance, for killers to eat and retire.

The work over time diminished, the miles behind them grew,
Their oars had been peaked, boats dragged behind, the wind blew,
Whale dragging, surf upon the bows, curling, sprouting outwards,
Surf to phosphorescent, day to night, stepping into the woods.

Approaching an unknown, coming fast, no star in the sky,
No moon to aid them, no pleasantness, all of this was to deny,
Though good it was that the weather was not out to destroy,
Wind fresh, slightly cold, but getting wet from water was no joy.

Jackets were placed on, more or less at the same time,
Some a little too small for the wearers, nothing to berhyme,
For when first they clambering aboard to give chase upon whale,
Each crew did go to incorrect boat, in decision they all did fail.

So long as oars were manned, a concern which did not atone,
For the cold now penetrated each and every one to the bone,
The wish for their own jackets on many of their mind,
To encase their bodies like a nut within shell, of orange in rind.

Discomfort did occur: men finding themselves seated at oar new,
New grip not used to: a seat change, though such cases were few,
No thrill to paw over an oar, but also no real call to complain,
Unaccustomed grip, not snug, not worn down by flesh on grain.

SONG OF THE OCEAN

And many years of handling also saw the seat fit snug,
Like flea finding home upon dog, nice, lush, as though in a rug,
It was strange how the mind worked, how familiarity was firm,
Firm as in secure, peace of mind, mind never to toil or to squirm.

It was a little different for headsman and harpooners,
Here there was command and structure, they were not learners,
Each had a specific task needing attention, a required need,
Which included changing positions, iron into whale to feed.

A boat's worth was in its commander,
Or not, for he is worthless without good lancer,
Mmm, yes, all were one, part of the team, one and the same,
Also individuals, and mannerisms of mind do tire of the game.

The occasional sign of the whale's intermittent exchange,
Between water haven and surface, his open range,
Was made all the clearer by the phosphorus display afore,
The rope tearing through water, same again, a constant encore.

The whale was making no sign of giving up the fight,
Surrender far from its mind, to do as he pleased, it was his right,
The killers commenced to feel as though they had bitten too much,
More than they could chew, out of their reality, out of touch.

But was it not the whale whom had placed himself upon menu,
Even gone as far as to choose the venue,
Waltzing into the comfortable and serene appeal of Twofold bay,
To endeavour, to try, for a short and comfortable stay.

ORCINUS ORCA

Now the whale insisted and had turned the power of the play,
The land far behind them, getting further and further away,
And before time they were 7.5 miles out to ocean as it beckoned,
Their momentum into the darkness didn't waver for a second.

George held his arms tight to chest when John's voice broke,
Slight terror to rise in mind, a vision beginning to smoke,
For the noise of the boats being dragged through the water,
Did advise, ropes crossed, George should cut his sooner, not later.

A sudden upheaval then delivered itself to the air,
A thunderous crash demanded a look, all to suddenly stare,
A sound which could be one thing and one thing only, right here,
John's boat, had been hit, smashed hard, hope gone, to disappear.

The smashing of boat reached their ears and Sam leapt too,
Leapt to action, tomahawk in hand, the line hit, cutting through,
Releasing the boat's connection with the prize that had showered,
Blossoms of spray amidst coercion of mind now empowered.

The members of the other crew had been cast into the ocean,
The whale turned back on the boat to create more commotion,
Smashing it hard with its flukes as it sounded briefly,
Then rose again beneath them, killing Peter Lia immediately.

Mass of fluke falling upon him with great strength,
A fluke so large and of great length,
No warning, the continuing momentum of the downward force,
Splitting boat into two, whereupon it sank: separation, divorce.

SONG OF THE OCEAN

Mass of wood, lances, manila and thwarts, keg of water and more,
Rations and blond Norwegian, all drift helplessly to water's floor,
A man, always happy, his singing in the try-works, cheerful smile,
Where hard labour was always met, gone forever, now defile.

The work was now cut out for them and they had to act fast,
Water so cold that no one human life in it could last,
Cries for help appeared from out of nowhere,
The dark surrounds enveloping all, too much to bear.

A little phosphorus providing aid, someone was splashing about,
Some treading water, or swimming precariously without a shout,
All trying to get closer to the only boat afloat, their only scope,
The life saver to deliver eleven men to safety, to wish and hope.

A few of the killers then separated from the others, their pod,
To undertake a different task, immediately, without request or nod,
A task which went unnoticed by those in the water staying afloat,
Either plashing about or at safe harbour in their little green boat.

Under the sway of Big Ben, having now taken command,
Cooper, Tom, Hooky, Jackson, and Sharkey did understand,
Took positions around the scene to protect and to serve,
To aid the men they knew so well, as they all did deserve.

It was clear to the killers that they were far out to ocean,
That sharks might be about, not far from vicinity and action,
The last thing Stranger, or any of the others, did wish,
Was for their allies to be picked off by shark, a most tasty dish.

ORCINUS ORCA

One by one the men were drawn out of the ice cold water,
Drenched, utterly and completely, but held from slaughter,
Chill of ocean devouring energy, this boat now their sumpter,
Depriving them of good spirit, their thoughts with friend Peter.

And the ring or orca surrounding the boat,
Was maintained during the ordeal to stay afloat,
From climbing aboard the vessel of desire,
Till onwards to bay, and killers did retire.

But the bay was a long way off, still no disclosure,
And the killing of whale had not been their pleasure,
Although Orcinus, one and all, did return to the excitement,
Back into the fray and the frenzy, for victories achievement.

The gunwale of the boat was barely above the surface,
So dangerously close to being sunk, in that, no solace,
And the saviour of the day, other than the orca in time of need,
That the ocean was still calm, the sun appearing, warmth to feed.

The sun on the horizon, began to shed light,
Gone was the torment, gone was some blight,
But weight of death was still on their shoulder,
Each and everyone felt it, the strong and the bolder.

And with the sun came the ability to see around,
The waters around them, the far off vision of ground,
Of the poor flesh and bone, those plucked from the ocean,
Having been, that night, guided by voice, a magic potion.

SONG OF THE OCEAN

Positions in the boat were taken up, all,
Turn-taking at oars, still much work to fall,
Assurance and general comradeship providing a little relief,
Looking to sky, praying to God, no matter what their belief.

Instinct now took command and for the coast they rowed,
The whale they had forgotten, even as in the distance it bellowed,
They only thought now of the lights on shore, so far away,
Hoping for the water around them, below gunwale to stay.

After many hours of stroking the oars upon the watery grave,
And much time in thought and prayer, visions of church nave,
They came upon the sound of surf hitting the shore,
So close now, the entrance of bay, of Eden and home's door.

And Jim was on South Head, unlit lantern now in hand,
Waiting patiently for their return, there he did stand,
Saw from his vantage only one boat return,
Of the disaster he would soon learn.

As they drew into the bay,
Eleven men in a bad way,
Some worse off than others,
Wretched site, especially for mothers.

None would forget this day, enough to make drunk man sober,
The worst day that any of them could ever recall or remember,
Lost was Peter Lia and a sturdy boat, both now rest in grave,
Far below the surface of the waves rest Peter, Peter the brave.

ORCINUS ORCA

In memory of Peter a stone was erected,
No less could this have been expected,
An inscription dated September 28th, 1881, for all to see,
To Peter Lia, who was killed by a whale: there to always be.

As for the whale, we shall never know,
Did he manage, of the killers, to throw,
Did he indeed make his escape, clear and far,
Harpoon still embedded, the point forever to jar.

SONG OF THE OCEAN

THE MOTHER OF MARY

Far from Eden, far to the south,
Killers mingled freely, food to mouth,
Had stumbled upon a meagre minke whale of little delight,
Worth a play, but hardly worth the pleasure of fight.

And so Tom and the others broke off their quest,
Something caught their attention, thoughts on which to rest,
So, they were coming up from the rear of a steamer so grand,
SS Ly-ee-Moon, making its way towards Sydney land.

She was a steamer of great prestige and held in high esteem,
Built to be fast at 17 knots [20miles per hr], furnished to gleam,
Only the best that money could buy, looking so fine,
Initially built as a paddle steamer in 1859.

The ship measured 282 feet long and 27 wide,
Powered by a coal fed steam engine, over waters to glide,
Engines which turned the huge wheels, through water to power,
Within its pores, pride and prestige to seemingly shower.

She was originally rigged with three masts and fitted with sail,
Could make good speed where weather permitted, without fail,
Within 20 years [1878] was returned to service on modification,
By removal of mast, turned into schooner-rigged vessel of notion.

ORCINUS ORCA

There were few lights on board and all appeared alright,
Ship plodding along at leisurely pace to everyone's delight,
All on board completely unaware as to what lay ahead,
No ill-fate from such calm weather could be read.

She had departed Melbourne on Saturday 29 May, 1886,
All 55 passengers and a crew of 41, relaxed and freely mix,
Captain Webber having left control of vessel in another's care,
In that of James Fotheringhame, the Third Officer, mind aglare.

James, having been handed much responsibility, rather discreetly,
So he, the captain, could retire to cabin, drink taken neatly,
Pro: the weather, not bad; Fotheringham mature and understood,
Con: a drunk captain of high responsibility was by no means good.

Later: they were approaching Green Cape, lighthouse of 3 years,
A blinking in far distance, a warning across many miles, appears,
A signal 95 feet high, 144 feet from level of ocean,
Sat upon crest, for eleven miles its warning to take action.

'Stay clear, there are rocks about,
This warning to you I do shout,
Do not approach, do not come closer,
Rocks abound, the ships' eraser'.

At this time, curiosity was ablaze, unbeknown to those on board,
The killers of Big Ben's pod escorted the ship, a playful reward,
Vessel of beauty, over gentle rollers pass, soon to ocean bequeath,
The sleek, beautiful creatures, masters of death, swam beneath.

SONG OF THE OCEAN

White surf thrown up from the bow, music to the ear,
The sound of the ocean wasted upon night so young and clear,
And Green Cape was soon larger than life in the window,
James fighting concern for making hasty decision or fallow.

The captain had retired, orders made clear,
Do not wake him unless urgent, not to go near,
Green Cape was 16 miles shy of Twofold bay,
Leave me in cabin for a while, there to stay.

And the captain still sucked on the nipple,
Savouring his source and a snack to nibble,
Getting as drunk as a Lord,
This was the story, but not every word.

Tom could see as he spy-hopped a little, above water's lip,
A man stepping from bridge, towards stern of ship,
Throwing waste into the ocean as though to curse and spurn,
Unaware of the killers presence, still yet of little concern.

It was at this point that Fotheringhame made the hasty decision,
To call upon the services of the captain, to avoid any collision,
For him to be called to duty, James feeling inapt and fidge,
But the captain flatly refused to attend the matter on bridge.

After nine that night the captain returned quickly amidst dire call,
James seeing before him the drunkenness seemingly fall,
The sobering effect that plain rocks above ocean instills,
Is more empowering than one wishes or wills.

ORCINUS ORCA

But he was too late and the ship hit rocks,
At the half hour chime of clocks,
Tom and the others could not foresee the danger to fall,
The hunger of rocks ready to mill, ready to maul.

Far unlike the captain with his years of mounted experience,
Years wasted within minutes due to shear arrogance,
Stern upon reef and bow floating precariously towards the shore,
There was too little one could do, before them death's open door.

The dangerous predicament was out of all proportion,
The rocks of Green Cape beyond wildest imagination,
The fight for survival commenced as though violently thrust,
The adrenalin taking place over clear thinking, survival a must.

Lighthouse workers heard the commotion, the grinding of ship,
The vessel tearing up, a battle against rocks, it beginning to rip,
Daniel Whelan and George Walters coming to the assistance,
Of those in dire need, they made a swift appearance.

Tom and the others of the pod moved in a little but most sure,
Steady at first, maintaining good distance, hearts most pure,
For even with their skill and experience of the ocean,
The rocks proved to be treacherous and unyielding in motion.

The foremast upon the bow fell and landed upon rock,
Where seamen and others started to crawl to safety in shock,
A fishing line thrown to the ship on which was attached a rope,
A line of safety, security blanket, something in which to hope.

SONG OF THE OCEAN

With rope tied fast, Herbert Lumsdaine made for safety of land,
Rocks so savage, lighthouse aloft, ready and able to withstand,
Withstand the assault of all that nature had to offer him,
For life at that minute was like walk on edge of sword: grim.

Others followed beneath the line to safety, no easy lope,
Andrew Bergland, a passenger, Fotheringhame to follow on rope,
Making it to safety a further ten good people with boatswain,
Lastly the captain, only duty performed that night, it was plain.

One to die, Mrs Flora Hannah MacKillop, never again to saunter,
A legacy left behind in reminder of her most humble daughter,
Mother to Mary MacKillop, Mary: of figure and station,
Mother of Mother Superior of St Joseph's Provident Institution.

Needless of this, shall we speak of it more,
Of the killers and their trials, of their unspoken law,
Tom endeavouring to rescue some that clung to unsafe rock,
Whom fear for their lives, not knowing, he was not there to shock.

It was an effort, to attempt their very salvation,
Swimming as close as possible in this hopeless situation,
He being thrust helplessly against a formation of rock so large,
Some teeth knocked out, no shield against this, no [archaic] targe.

He retreated having secured, of this situation, no victory,
For it was too treacherous, a predicament of shear gravity,
And further screaming continued unabated for some of the night,
Twenty persons, upon stern, washed out to ocean, crying in fright.

ORCINUS ORCA

Give in, the pod did not, as Tom gave direction,
His attempts to rally all and employ relative salvation,
Tom is not the matriarch, not female, but is a strong peer,
His persona had won law of the tongue, so could win here.

A rescue attempt must be staged,
This war with the ocean must be waged,
Do here as they do with the green boats, their contribution,
Treat those who appear with the same gravitation.

And Tom could quite clearly recall how Peter Lia had died,
Killed by the flukes of the whale crushing boat, life denied,
How the body sank lifelessly towards the bottom of ocean floor,
Visual picture clear in his mind as it then disappeared, ever more.

Again and again the killers attempted to move in with aid,
Trying with all their effort, but the people were too afraid,
To help them to safety where possible was not coming about,
Do justice where deserved amidst people, they scream and shout.

The Davidson's had served them well over the past year,
In return they should do the same, this was fundamentally clear,
This society, these humans, were part of their pod,
Whether in ocean they swam or on land they trod.

Like brothers and sisters, they were intelligent,
Proved to be emotional and rather diligent,
Showed semblance in many respects of their own,
As though ancestral in some way, cognition ingrained, well sown.

SONG OF THE OCEAN

But still they feared the worst, that mental curse,
People preferred to remain upon sinking hearse,
To be dragged beneath the waves for that ever good night,
Fighting off the killers where one strayed too close: such spite.

And so many lives were lost unnecessarily, 71 to be exact,
Three of which were very young children, but does not detract,
Not detract from the overall numbers that died at Green Cape,
A loss that could have been avoided: of death, life to escape.

And so the killers swam off as the moon rose above the horizon,
To swim once more towards Leather Jacket Bay and good reason,
To head off a whale heard swimming near, large morsel indeed,
A large monster of a mammal on which to chase and to feed.

With distinct probability that others, would appear, other pods,
To aid them in their hunt with intelligence and teeth, not rods,
To then congregate prior to approaching Twofold Bay and glory,
To further furnish their memory with another hunting story.

And a surprise was found to be awaiting them as news fell,
Humpy had returned to the pod, one she had known so well,
Returned with her son, Walker, who was barely one year old,
Who would become just a number, never a legend nor bold.

It was strange she should return alone: had never been needy,
But it was not possible for Humpy to portray the tragedy,
A tragedy that unfolded during a clash with a humpback whale,
One with a calf that refused to die, to fight for calf in this vale.

ORCINUS ORCA

Typee, her mate, had taken a fluke directly in the side,
Which was enough to split him open, too much to bide,
An uncommon and freak occurrence, sad to recall,
Typee died soon after, his life had come to its end, to stall.

Humpy had no real choice but to return to Eden and stability,
Leaving behind fond memories, but an estranged community,
Who treated her with defiance, no gratitude for hunting ability,
Treated poorly, no time for her majestic and athletic agility.

Humpy's time away from home was a reflection of her mind,
Cared not to recall, to search it corridors for importance to find,
She was here now, with calf, and Typee was gone to never return,
Walker to be looked after, accepted, one she could never spurn.

SONG OF THE OCEAN

THE GREATEST AID

By the 1890s, G.Davidson, formerly known as Fearless George,
Had taken over the family business, mind built as of a forge,
Relying on ingenuity for survival during the off season,
Easy to see why he ran a small farm: good sense, good reason.

But where winter was waited upon, so the rewards were set,
A reward close to shore: fishing done with lance, not with net,
Tongue and lips for Orcinus, mammals, full of power and might,
Casks of oil for men of the land, not as cunning but very bright.

The relationship between the two species continued to evolve,
Problems and initiative, always a way, always something to solve,
When Orcinus became tangled in ropes, the men lent a hand,
When man was bound by water and shark, Orcinus would stand.

And so here we speak, of all things that evolved, of all to meet,
One was to be remembered forever, a memory to warmly greet,
The day killers had ventured into the bay, warning men ashore,
A humpback within distance, seemingly on leisurely tour.

Two other pods were shaken from nap,
Set into motion regards setting of trap,
Now patrolling the mouth of the bay,
In the hope that the whale would stay.

ORCINUS ORCA

This great fish, required use of men's hands for impeding,
To aid in bringing her down, for pods to have their feeding,
Preferred the quick kill as opposed to the drawn out,
To hence set upon, green boats to launch with almighty shout.

Tom lead the way and all three commenced flop-tailing, their best,
Leaping from the water, hitting it hard, waking men from rest,
The unmistakable sound of calling traversing far and wide,
A beacon to secure the interests of man, calling him to tide.

Call the men to duty, to express without any doubt,
That there was a whale in their midst, waiting about,
One to be had, but it would not wait all night,
And from the dark depths of cabin, men stirred for the fight.

Men lying, in heavenly, blissful sleep, now a stirred commotion,
Dreams lost, alcoholic stupors torn, all clambered for position,
Shredding men of slumber and cloud-soft beds, no treason,
But happily stricken of the fear of a 'fruit and whale-less' season.

RUSHO! That unmistaken beating of drum, the sound and shrill,
Unmistaken command and call to duty, a hard to swallow pill,
There had been a heavy night of the spirits, drinks going around,
Commissary in misery, but now justice to be found.

Though only half the men managed to make it to the boats,
For they would not wait for the slow: George not taking votes,
Words strung to extricate more power, each to heave,
If unable to work under trying conditions then it was time to leave.

SONG OF THE OCEAN

But men loved this work, enjoyed the hell,
Working the try-works, but not the beastly smell,
So give arms to the task they do, pull the oars under their charge,
Hit task hard with effort, not to gently tickle, like fairies sparge.

George, as a student, looked towards the heavens above,
Studied his book before compiling a work he did love,
Looking to crystal ball, to the hours which lay ahead,
To foresee the weather of hours ahead, to be clearly read.

There was a half moon and sparse cloud spanning across the sky,
A westerly strong breeze, the ocean calm, on good weather to rely,
By all appearances they were in for an easy night,
But what of the whale? Would it be an easy fight?

Rising from the darkness the rowers then heard the familiar sound,
Of a humpback whale in the midst, of its demise inward bound,
A little further out upon the ocean, the pods and their hounding,
And the killers could hear the green boats, their oars pounding.

Tom remained at the stern having gained the men's attention,
Now leading the way, his phosphorus showing the direction,
The light from the moon hiding behind the occasional cloud,
A bond, friends of sea and land, something in which to be proud.

Tom came to the side of the boat, and time held much essence,
He needed the men, and men he, each other required that presence,
More so than not for there was only one boat here this night,
To do the work of two or three, and now with the lack of light.

ORCINUS ORCA

He sideswiped the boat gently from beneath, oars pushed aside,
Drawing the attention of whalers as though asking for ride,
Eyes falling upon the mass, dorsal stretched out towards the sky,
A fin then struck them with fear, possessing such power, not shy.

Queries passed between breathes as they went for the prize,
Questions on his behaviour: would the boat capsize,
Would they all end up in the sea, thrashing to stay afloat,
To be hampered, lives taken, heads bitten off at the throat.

And the then one of the seated declared a solution as done before,
Tom Earl allowing a chuckle upon lips, inwards vision he saw,
Suggesting they throw him the painter [short rope] at the bow,
To see whether or not he was offering assistance, the boat to tow.

George looked inquisitively upon the suggestion and upon Tom,
Who was growing anxious, annoyed at slow progress, a bomb,
Tom feared the humpback would make its escape to deeper water,
That the youngest of the pod would not survive the winter.

They were all hungry but preferred to remain at Twofold Bay,
For the aid provided by the men and stick of iron, silvery grey,
There, dissension in their group, mothers concerned for the young,
But one good whale would provide enough, death hence sprung.

The killer hit the flank again, oars in danger, a possible loss,
George then gave the nod for harpooner, the painter to toss,
To see once and for all what Tom would do with the rope,
To see if the killer was in fact giving them hope.

SONG OF THE OCEAN

The harpooner's face drew a collection of eyeballs, enthralled,
Looks falling upon the dark man, oar no longer pulled,
Oar lifted temporarily from water, for the painter he did reach,
Threw it into the water, to see if Tom was there to teach.

Jaws dropped then with the forward motion of the boat and Tom,
The killer opened his mouth, taking the rope as though to bosom,
A gentle grasp before pulling them over wave, the way so paved,
Clear access to humpback now granting them time, much saved.

This was a scene to remember, one for the books,
An incident never to be forgotten, but not escaping sour looks,
For many would not believe this, but the experience was grand,
One of the greatest feats of man and beast, not achieved on land.

The two killers that were with Tom looked upon his manner ,
Of action, mystic, the status of legend called to his banner,
But for Tom this was no time for fun,
He had a duty to perform, there was work to be done.

The boat was making good headway now, better than before,
Yet still the men rowed, true conviction, much sweat to pour,
But this killer whale, this Orcinus Orca, so brave, not naive,
Had done what no other could do, so much he did achieve.

Whistles, clicks and calls filled the ocean, it woken from slumber,
Echolocation, their repertoire of calls was quite large in number,
Sounds made when chasing a whale, commands to obey,
Signals, clear signs to adhere, the reaping of harvest, their prey.

ORCINUS ORCA

The sonic signatures of the acoustic communication,
Consisted of pitch, harmonic structure, oscillation,
Tone, urgency, mood, loudness and action,
All an aid, enabled the killers to kill, the great tactician.

Sometimes employing click trains as opposed to singular clicks,
Dependent on the type of prey hunted, depended on their tricks,
Marine mammals could pick up on these, no dilapidating manner,
Where fish could not, as though into works was fed a spanner.

Passive listening was simply an extension of their abilities,
Sound commands and requests the strongest of strategies,
Straight conversation, calls indicating species and pod members,
That's all was needed, that's all there was, from their very fibres.

The very effort and commotion of the fight to keep,
The whale in the bay, of escape in waters deep,
And with this the boat nears its final approach, to close,
Upon this humpbacks daily life, a face-off, almost nose to nose.

The whale gave an almighty effort to escape the clutches of all,
Turning upon the teeth infected mouths, never to be in thrall,
An herculean effort surfacing, its raging scorn,
To be more than he could, to be the greatest thorn.

Great strength erupting like a volcano from its every sinew,
From every fibre burst an amassed energy, outwards it blew,
But escape? A humpback could only muster 7.5 miles an hour,
The killer could go 18: though at 100 a day and it began to sour.

SONG OF THE OCEAN

Tom dropped the rope now, to join in the grind,
The importance of the game growing clear upon his mind,
A further escort of three killers joining in the final fray,
The humpback now coming towards boat, harpooner to pray.

The harpooner got ready in an instant for a frontal shot,
Another notch on his belt secured: if missed, then not,
Seeing the large mass of black coming full steam ahead,
The gap closing fast, harpooner hoping to put this to bed.

The headsman grasped the steering oar with both hands,
Pulled this into chest, further bracing as he kneels then stands,
Leaning back and stabilising himself as best he could,
Harpooner slightly askew, whale coming upon boat of wood.

The harpooner stood then, not too late, not too soon,
Cloud moving, most temporarily, in front of the moon,
Now sudden realization, the humpback, oneself did expose,
The harpooner struck hard, iron in head, straight for the nose.

Released a good throw that penetrated deep and stuck well,
The 'fast fish' was made, darkened moon no evil spell,
The harpooner had secured a good line for lancing to start,
Thinking himself proud, a great harpooner, possibly smart.

The whole issue of fight and slander had worked to a means,
Their purses to fill with colour of money, not magical beans,
Even before the try-pots could boil the blubber of carcass won,
He was counting his chickens, such victory, such hazardous fun.

ORCINUS ORCA

But the humpback did not see this to his front,
And so reared its head, a tremendous brunt,
His head, broad and rounded, as from the top you saw,
A rounded protuberance beneath the tip of the lower jaw.

Fleshy knobs of barnacle covering most of its head,
Where blowhole sat a spouting, but not of red,
The vapours were of that reddish tinge so often sought,
Flew seven feet into the air and whale still far from caught.

Thrashing from side to side, back now arching, whale much alive,
The flukes coming up towards the surface in preparation to dive,
Seen here was a small dorsal fin, two-thirds down its back,
A nubbin of little consequence, of no importance should we stack.

Water fell upon them from beneath the crushing flukes, dissipated,
A convex shaped surge of surf that was disassociated,
Disassociated from the calm of the ocean, or of the sea,
A separate entity with one concern and one concern only there be.

To drench those within the boat, men who belong on shore,
To soak the wearers of jacket and shirt to the very core,
And gasps of shock erupted from their mouths, none alone,
As the cold of the water hit home, to the very bone.

The stabbing of the ocean's dousing driving home as it can,
That the waters around were dangerous, no playground for man,
Horrors now bland, stillness mused to come over the ocean wave,
The whale and the killers had disappeared, from sight they cave.

SONG OF THE OCEAN

Several men surrendered their oars and quickly emptied the boat,
Bailing out water, all amazed that they were still afloat,
Working fast and furious to the best of their ability,
Before returning back to oars, their command, their duty.

The surface then erupted once more into a flurry,
The body masses of all involved surfaced again in a hurry,
The harpooner then changed positions with headsman real fast,
Lancing to commence immediately, hopefully not to last.

All of a sudden silence fell over them again,
And once more all appeared and seemed to be in vain,
Nothing but the cloud in the sky and the light of the moon,
The sea and its stabbing cold, but they had thought too soon.

By the time George took the stern the fighting was in full swing,
Two species of whale beneath, a ballet, a fight, to herald and sing,
Great chunks of blubber torn from the humpback, a near tonne,
But the fight below the surface was far from won.

The humpback was trying to head for deeper water,
To make for an escape, away from the slaughter,
And again they surfaced, surges of water, the oars pulled in,
Bursts of fury, a fight most furious, upon man not a single grin.

The killers were rallying together,
This their strength, their strongest tether,
Their ability to work as a team, providing support,
The orca swarmed from all sides, their frantic effort.

ORCINUS ORCA

As the green boat continued to maintain its visual connection,
The strengthening of the humpbacks desire, a resurrection,
The harpoon still secure for the minute but lancing stalled,
Orca did all they could to hamper an escape, unabatedly mauled.

Killers threw themselves upon the blowhole of whale,
Others snatched on to lips without fail,
Ripping chunks from its bulk, Tom taking another bite,
With bites from fins and fluke, from any site.

In another effort to throw the assault into affray,
The humpback dived and turned, as though to stray,
The harpoon line falling slack, a bad omen, bad fate,
An order to counter the turn, for all to hear, came too late.

The movement of the rope and boat had caught George's leg,
Into the calm ocean he toppled, a tough man, who does not beg,
But the stabbing cold had knocked the wind from him most clean,
Like never before, the watery surrounds, its endeavour to demean.

Sam and Albert sprang to life and commenced to cut the line free,
Allow the humpback small victory: one they would likely not see,
The large mass of humpback heading away from them now,
Time of the essence, to aid George, somewhere near the bow.

For what seemed an eternity the headsman was being dragged,
Beneath the surface, no longer encumbered by rope, not snagged,
Of the cut rope George now fought his way clear,
Removed weight of shoes and jacket, for panic did smear.

SONG OF THE OCEAN

Smear his judgement but not his cause,
To fight for survival, not to give in, not to pause,
He worked himself to he surface where the light from the moon,
Brought great slathers of relief and not too soon.

The boat was more than four football fields away,
He now alone, far from rescued, bobbing around, to gently sway,
The solace of ocean this minute forgotten, unlike unkind remarks,
As he tread water in order to stay afloat, he thought: sharks!

Cowards they were, one and all, these heinous carnivores,
Scared to death of Orcinus, no matter where one takes its tours,
But drawn to the actions of their fight for food, like a spell,
They come running, remain at distance, to this ringing of bell.

Nothing like supping on the remains of a humpback,
Whether a great meal or simply a snack,
Scroungers to devour and take what they need,
No opportunity passed on when, or where, to feed.

And where to find sharks of the ocean,
Forever on the move, forever in motion,
Everywhere, anywhere, an encumbrance of the deep,
Of water and shore, allowing them to take, to forever reap.

George could feel their presence,
He was sure of it, the very essence,
And then it came upon his ears, the disturbance of the surface,
Amidst the swirling of the sea, that dread, life to efface.

ORCINUS ORCA

He was at more risk of death now, than ever before,
Alone in the water and so far from shore,
No boat by his side and no knife to ward off an intruder,
Dark annals of the waters about him, lurking was a marauder.

His eyes popped from his skull as a fin came into view,
Heading for him on a slight angle, closer it drew,
The unmistakable mast of a shark on the prowl,
No audible warning: no snarl from lion, or from bear a growl.

But what was this? Something thrown into the mix,
More fin rose; NO! A dorsal! Shear remedy to fix,
And the knob atop the fin… damn, it was hard to see,
Yes indeed, it was; it was Tom: Oh, glory be.

But was he to be relied upon,
Tom was like a formidable weapon,
He was a double-edged sword,
Either single or an orca horde.

Tom then filled George with slight dread,
A little terror upon face of George easily read,
He knew killers were more menacing than sharks ever were,
Shark feared killer, so killer was most feared, with wrath to incur.

No shark ever interfered with the joys of a killer whale,
As it fed upon its victims, this no myth or fairy tale,
Was Tom, who he knew, from the safety of his green boat,
Here to take him in jaws, crunch him like a peanut, then to gloat.

SONG OF THE OCEAN

Many times had George seen a killer take on a shark or two,
Or seen one take on a whale so enormous and large, it was true,
By all comparison, that before him now was beyond all belief,
He imagined the worst, what it could do to him, and be so brief.

Tom looked upon this man, seeing George close up and personal,
Bobbing there, up and down, a salmon ready to take, to maul,
George grew more tense, the beast, closing the gap ever more,
It swam around him, George watched, to clarify what he saw.

He consoled himself, Tom would leave him be, not toy and eat,
Not tear him like rag, drawn into throat, eternal doom to meet,
And the minutes would tell, but safety then threw a lifeline,
For the cloud above gave sight to moon, a sight so fine.

Releasing itself from the clouds so high in the sky,
The green boat and its crew, he could not deny,
Out of the darkness, as a knight to the rescue,
The men at arms, the chivalrous, the ones he loved and knew.

And as spoken, George then saw friendship in Tom's eye,
Tom nodding his head, a gesture, no exaggeration, no lie,
And so with the shark having fled and George soon to be safe,
Tom returned to the fight against whale, to harass, to chafe.

The boat then drew alongside as he knew it would,
Plucked him, wrapped him in blanket as fast as they could,
The experience was unbelievable, this great monster of the sea,
Protector most friendly and warm, most humble and free.

ORCINUS ORCA

He had surrendered himself until George was safe from harm,
Despite initial terror and within his head the ringing of alarm,
Had aided him until rescued by the others of his entourage,
So lucky he were for this experience, this stirring, by and large.

Tom was indeed a good friend,
There to aid, to help, to defend,
George almost a meal for a shark,
But light was drawn from the dark.

Tom then returned to his pod under Big Ben, most worthy,
Big Ben recalled how they protected men before, did agree,
How they protected them in their case of flesh, to assist,
But Tom had taken it to the next level, new contract to persist.

It seemed nothing more than stupidity to get so close to the men,
With danger looming, all so tense and fragile, but slightly uneven,
Tom could have been seen as the threat, men acting against him,
Skewered by harpoon and lance as he did protect, as he did swim.

Tom felt as though there was more than a common connection,
That there existed a greater understanding, just short of perfection,
Men served them, aiding the hunt, gifted them lip and tongue,
Ever since the Yuin of years past, worshipers and heroes unsung.

And so Tom had laid this question or immortal aid and law,
A foundation on which to continue the build, strong with no flaw,
They each seemed to have a better understanding of one another,
The bond between them strengthened, never to break or to suffer.

SONG OF THE OCEAN

THE WHITE HEATHER

In 1901, 19 killer whales returned: Stranger, Youngster, Walker,
Big Ben, Tom, Hooky, Jimmy, Little Jack, Cooper,
Humpy, Jackson, Skinner, Charlie Adgery, Sharkey,
Big Jack, Young Ben, Albert, Kinscher, Brierly.

The humpback population would receive a reprieve this year,
Though still numerous in number, with this security does appear,
Easy pickings for the three pods working the numbers,
Pods under Stranger, Big Ben and Humpy, rope's core not fibres.

But bad news upon the horizon did show its ugly head,
Norwegian whalers in Australian waters putting resource to bed,
Shooting quite openly, Orcinus as they swam harmlessly about,
Clarified by Norwegians boasting, recklessly and with loud shout.

Norwegians concerned that the orca would eat their Godly ware,
Taking money from their pockets, more than their fare share,
A demoralising dilemma staining the traits of man, his ignorance,
Such so that the Yuin were moving from Eden and sustenance.

And so gone is a commodity of people, hard workers strong,
Annoyed by the whalers and all they did that was wrong,
Norwegian whalers, employing motors not oars,
A grievance and mistrust, insult to Orcinus and their laws.

ORCINUS ORCA

For Tom it wasn't so much as a requirement to survive,
After so many years it was more about feeling alive,
With the aid of man they had learnt to thrive,
To collaborate with men on surface, or with pod in a dive.

They cooperated with the crews, the men of the green boats,
For the pleasure of the chase, of the hunt, a feeling that bloats,
For the thrill of the kill, part of human life, this magic potion,
People that walked on land, and also swam in the ocean.

During the final stages of Davidson's enterprise, do not deny,
With cost of oil falling, bay whaling was starting to die,
A friend named J.R.Logan aided the green by towing to ocean,
In reach of baleen by use of White Heather, poetry in motion.

White Heather, a yacht of lines and pleasure,
A joy to watch and to sail a great leisure,
To tow the row boats quite happily to where they need,
To the scene of the hunt, oil to harvest, orca to feed.

The use of silent and effective hand-thrown harpoon and lance,
Still great commodity employed, securing a kill, a good chance,
But the affection was the most formidable feeling, a golden gem,
Orcinus feeling more for the crews than the crews felt for them.

And this is the way it was all of those years ago,
Good memories to pour sour, mournful memories soon to sow,
Though for the present they apt to do as they could,
To hunt together as Tom knew they would.

THE FAILURE

The passing of George's father came in 1903,
Memories flooding back, scenes easy to see,
Dreams filled with the laughter and fighting spirit,
Whaling will continue, his life worthy of great merit.

The hunt must continue hence reflections held back,
Personal ruminations not permitted to stack,
For the mind was a fragile place, subtle, easy to cave,
No place for this on the ocean, thrashed by wind and wave.

George looked over the men in the boat as they rammed the bow,
Into the little surf that sprang up before them, high then low,
Each breaking upon the sleekness of their tool-of-the-trade,
Seemingly unbreakable, far from truth, though sturdily made.

He lapsed most temporarily upon his father,
Then saw the characters of those to the front in lather,
Another boat could be heard as it too entered surging wave,
The water encountered with a thud by the brave.

The men before him, stroking the sea with their oars,
As they knew how, harnessing strength from their very pores,
their backs were facing him as he came upon them from the stern,
Men of adventure, of ocean, men one-and-all, never to spurn.

ORCINUS ORCA

Most were becoming old men with failing gears,
Not just in age but also through the tally of years,
Where hard-yakka piled on the age in double helpings,
Two serves for one, harsh upon the body, but a good innings.

Charlie, Archer [George's brother] and Boyd,
Boyd not to be confused with the opposition, no semblance toyed,
Each long in the tooth but on each George could rely,
Being satisfied with all men, the crews, where courage does lie.

And from the corner of his eye he caught glimpses of shadow,
Noises from afar reached his ear, shallow and narrow,
His senses heightened as he peruse the shore and bay around,
Looking for his opposition: Boyd and Glover to be found.

Both were as keen as he to see a 'fast fish' secured all the more,
Crews filled with ambition, to press their every muscle to the oar,
But there was more strength in character, persistence, ambition,
Than in the strength of muscles, sinew, tissue or perspiration.

Glover could be seen approaching from upon the flank,
Slightly behind George and his two boats: if only they sank,
But the competition wouldn't let up, not throw in the towel,
They might break an oar, but wouldn't quit, trying not to fail.

But George had the orca up his sleeve, his joker,
Of one thing he had learnt it was how to play poker,
For humpbacks and rights were all unpredictable,
Though with the killer's cooperation all was more stable.

SONG OF THE OCEAN

The men continued to lean into the work, sweat-sodden shirts,
Their backs breaking as they asserted their Achilles efforts,
Muscle of character tearing up water, power, golden gilt,
Conviction of sustained power over every inch and yard spilt.

This was commandeering action, one learnt over many a year,
For it was an unknown, how many days or weeks would appear,
Before opportunity arose once more, to display how they felt,
Display this fortitude built of steel, dealing all that could be dealt.

With sudden realisation and the clarity of the chase racing back,
Falling upon their minds in flashes and splashes of black,
Ocean shrouding their boats, confetti upon glimmering wave,
The humpback bursting from ocean, no way to escape the grave.

The humpback majestically lifted itself from the watery tomb,
Only the flukes embalmed as though still connected to womb,
To crash back upon the ocean, to be greeted by Orcinus orca,
Killer throwing itself over the blowhole, a menace, a stalker.

The horror struck faces of the men in the green boat,
Was surreal, for such a scene was rare, so up close and afloat,
Time seemed to pause, or to simply slow down,
This action before their very eyes, whale of renown.

Orders to the rowers were issued amidst calmness and ease,
Loud bellows surely heard over theatre of war as it did tease,
But some men were haphazardly slow and oars bore the brunt,
Oars breaking, a whale gone crazy, thrash of body to their front.

ORCINUS ORCA

Sam Haddigaddi paused for a second before thrusting a harpoon,
Thrust with much power, iron of death, not too late, not too soon,
Departing his calloused hand another oar snapped like toothpick,
Sam thinking he had broken his arm with throwing of iron stick.

The squelch of point entering the whale, unnoticed by all around,
All but the whale that bore the brunt of the throw, heard the sound,
For the noise went raking across and cascaded down his back,
Deafening at the least, this terrifying assault, this blatant attack.

Every throw was the same, no matter the whale, the species,
The heart-wrenching threat, Death calling for death, no mercies,
The agony of knowing was the worst but fight on he would,
Even if drowned, by hand of man or devils of ocean as it stood.

But fight he did and continued with a great spurting of energy,
Coalesced force so supernatural, a drawing from pores, a synergy,
Racing towards the face of the cliff which overhung ocean wide,
Turning abruptly, melee entered, killers and men, side by side.

How it stood: the channel to freedom not open to the humpback,
He turned again towards the cliff, powerful flukes it did not lack,
And the killers felt as though the time had come, once and for all,
To finish off this beast of beasts, a death he did strenuously stall.

With pure suddenness the humpback disappeared under the water,
The green boat turned as though upon a leisurely saunter,
And the whale began to surface with the boat upon its back,
The men jostling for hold of the fragile shell upon mass of black.

SONG OF THE OCEAN

As the head of the whale began to surface and the boat to slide,
George leapt to feet without second thought, and leapt to side,
Landing upon the whale's back, as though meaning to ride,
Before pushing up again so hard, back to boat, on thwart astride.

The looks upon the men spoke more than words ever could,
And for briefest of moments the entire world sang as it should,
That the name Fearless George was humble, had true meaning,
And the chase then continued with smiles on men all gleaming.

Demise of their situation then bit hard,
The humpback refusing to give a yard,
Would not fall victim to the whims of either killers nor man,
A last ditch effort made once more, a cunning, malicious plan.

Instinct to survive, so strong within this creature beneath the skies,
Now seemingly up to the killers to bring about his final demise,
This mass of blubber trying to escape the snapping of jaw,
Orca only wishing to feed, to bring whale into a ravenous maw.

With one last ditch effort the killers forced, quite undeniably,
The humpback upon the rocks near South Head, most inevitably,
Where the last breaths of life fused in rapid action, then ceased,
Panic and torment having taken its toll, of life the whale released.

It was a sad state of affairs for both man and beast,
For the carcass was going nowhere, to be had no feast,
Out of reach of the killer's mouths and in difficult surrounds,
For the securing of blubber, no, for it was out of bounds.

ORCINUS ORCA

There was no need to anchor and buoy the carcass as usual,
No need to wait for the gases to re-float that sunken from visual,
This predicament out of the ordinary, upon the rocks to stay,
No easy access to secure the blubber and hence nothing to pay.

What God gives with one hand he takes with the other,
And in respect to this dilemma, it did nothing but smother,
It did suffocate their morale, for the whale was going nowhere,
Not able to tow it into harbour, almost too much to bear.

The mass would have to be deblubbered where it lay,
Upon the rocks of the shore where it stubbornly did stay,
From beneath the cliff, no afternoon sunshine, out of luck,
Where blasts from a westerly wind lashed, relentlessly struck.

It was here, amongst the rocks, the surf, and heavy wave,
Making strong legs unstable, stability upon brittle stave,
Strength drained like sorrows of a drunkard on bar stall,
To suffer this burden, to do all they could, to answer the call.

And the men looked out across the ocean on occasion,
Where swells further out crest higher, poor weatherly fashion,
A storm brewing, turning sour, to fill all hope with scorn,
Forcing fingers to work harder still, to bone seemingly torn.

They all knew well that they had several hours of work ahead,
But did not know how long it would last, this could not be read,
The crashing of waves upon them and the rocky outcrop,
The angry ocean growing in ferocity and anger, it would not stop.

SONG OF THE OCEAN

It was as though Poseidon by name and by justice,
Angered by the taking of creature, from the ocean did notice,
Not pleased the humpback should be cut into chunks and strips,
To have its body slashed, to be melted down, and for orca no lips.

Further out the killers congregated and swam in a circle,
Annoyed to hilt, a meal of sustenance denied them, an oracle,
Men weren't to blame; and neither was it the fault of the ocean,
The damn whale, beached upon the rocks, to deny: its ambition.

The killers gave to spy-hopping and watched the men work,
Men securing the catch as best they could, all frowning, no smirk,
Tools ferried from the try-works and the carving had begun,
Blubber caked the rocks, sheaves of white, dreary, lack of sun.

But Poseidon was to gift them something special, a reward,
For with the storm came another opportunity, one not to hoard,
A call received further out, a whale bypassing their position,
A sperm whale with calf further out to sea, a grand commission.

An uncommon occurrence which grew scarcer each year,
An offering so good, less and less did such appear,
Extinction caused by man and his incessant need,
Man's unwavering destruction, his almighty greed.

But a mother and calf,
That was a meal and half,
And for the joy of taste and chase,
They swam to stare it in the face.

ORCINUS ORCA

The signal came again, the calf being of reasonable size,
The pack of killers would do well to swim and receive their prize,
The sperm and her calf were on a course away from the pack,
The killers sure to catch up and by morning's first light be back.

To the sperm whale there was no real concern,
For the killers were so far away, but she would soon learn,
Yet she would maintain an open ear, pursue her purpose, her need,
Her quest for warmer waters, to feed, maintain her good speed.

The Hawaii Islands were a long way, she knew the waters well,
Knew of great abundances of food, delight on which to dwell,
And with her attention turned fully once more to the path ahead,
She moved amidst the noise of ocean and creatures of ocean bed.

Orca, on the hunt, dangerous and hungry, to deliver their skill,
To sink teeth into the best blubber of all, for them more than a kill,
To rip at the calf, a manipulative action, before resighting,
Then setting sights upon the mother, to continue their fighting.

It wouldn't be easy, for the female would hinder their every move,
Give her all to secure survival of her young, with much to prove,
But try as she might the killers would win their prize,
They would receive their fill, a mother of substantial size.

By this time the men upon the rocks had completed their task,
With no time to waste, no time to scratch: or for unpleasant bask,
And soon with their oars in the water they were going along,
The weather growing in its ferocity, sapping all feeling of song.

SONG OF THE OCEAN

Mounting waves of surging white crashing with great intent,
Upon the place where the humpback's remains were spent,
Now washed into the ocean as though a gaping mouth so great,
A small meal for the smallest of fish to have a measly treat.

And crab would take their share, seagulls would make their move,
All creatures and critters of ocean and coast now in the groove,
Move now for a delay would see the storm wash all so far away,
So all who were to sup, joined in the feeding, a scandalous fray.

ORCINUS ORCA

THE RIDE

The proprieties of bay whaling in 1904 were tasteless and stale,
The dashed ambitions of men, the infrequent appearance of whale,
The costs: good money required to run a bunkhouse full of men,
To run several boats and household, a luxury now and then.

It is true that idleness breeds dissatisfaction and discontent,
That sitting back with nought to do did not pay the rent,
Unable to afford the luxury of butter on bread,
With inappropriate behaviour so coloured and always dread.

Drink was permitted but not something one could easily atone,
Gambling an inbred vacuum sucking pockets as dry as a bone,
Most often winnings lost the following week, so weak the hold,
And pay was seldom offered until an harvest was sold.

So when the time comes for the call to be made,
Rousing itself from the roll of the tongue and easily laid,
Men jump into boats wrapped in layers of warmth, in comfort,
Scampering for thwarts and oars of their beloved with effort.

They do so with such urgency, as though the entire town is on fire,
And they the only firemen for miles around, their speed most dire,
For not only were they in competition with others of similar mind,
But in a timely chase against the hands of clock: don't fall behind.

SONG OF THE OCEAN

For every breath was a milestone,
Every humpback, oil and bone,
Quite often escaping, easily lost,
Amidst winds laden with heavy frost.

These men did not serve by way of a written contract,
Meagre wages not secured if there was no resource to extract,
But were paid with what the headsman could suckle from buyers,
Always quoting low prices, the best of the best, true liars.

In some cases this was substantial: no rich path to pave,
Even though prices rose and fell like the ocean wave,
But most rewarding of all was the work conducted,
A group of men toiling: a team well orchestrated.

Even so the men would not abandon their captain,
Knew there would be no riches flowing from fountain,
And wages paid islanders, whites, half-castes and aborigines,
Was the same all round: no racist boundaries, drawing of lines.

And so men sit at table, playing cards, hunched over a cup of tea,
When all of a sudden the call comes from aloft a horse at spree,
The beast breathing heavily and being ridden so hard,
Towards men awaiting call of RUSHO, word sung from bard.

A poetic call to action, for nothing else mattered this minute,
Crowd of men crossing cobbles in a sprint, each filled with spirit,
The ground around shook, the bustling steps, thundering of sound,
Call to boats, fresh morning air doused in mist, action to astound.

ORCINUS ORCA

Individuals clambered aboard their boat with quickened ease,
Oars picked up and thrust into position, anxieties to increase,
Surface of the bay quickly stroked to propel them ever forward,
Towards prize yet unclear, beyond visual, fathom, inch and yard.

And then the spouting caught the eye of George so assuredly,
Two humpbacks, beasts hounded by dogs of the sea most forcedly,
The wolves of the water, encumbrance of the baleen,
Devils of the murky surrounds, black and white, out to demean.

They were the evil at the backs of angels,
The shackles of torment, abusive bangles,
Of the earth and sky great eagles,
Above all, the dorsal of death that mangles.

The two humpbacks, forced towards the boats amidst whale song,
Driven towards the battle of wills, and the will of man is strong,
A man is stronger than Orcinus for he is willing to die,
Would readily give up his life in order for his children to fly.

Where a killer whale would only stress itself to its limits,
Lacking that understanding, or inability, or lacking spirit,
A man will fight to the death, with all his strength and might,
A killer would fall back, conserve its energy, give up the fight.

And so Harpoons and lances were struck and stuck,
The two whales secured within an hour of fighting, such luck,
Two boats and sidekicks fight, two species against humpback,
Each of medium size, but still a great victory, a great attack.

SONG OF THE OCEAN

They were both good kills, secured within good time,
And relief fell from the men's eyes as though doused in lime,
For their purses now had something, no longer a vacant berth,
Even if for only a short time, that magic paper of great worth.

The drought had been watered, the show was now on the road,
A great and heavy burden lifted from their shoulders, a sour load,
Everyone thought how lucky they were with this good fortune,
Of two such quick kills, one after the other, the lifting of evil rune.

And without thought the humpbacks were anchored and buoyed,
Killers taking their reward as usual, to east they deployed,
The men to return on the morrow to bring home the bacon,
But something was brewing, further out, something well shaken.

That night the winds blew as the men slumbered well,
The heavens being shaken by the very cores of hell,
As strong wind wakes deeply embedded roots of a gigantic tree,
For three days the weather grew against the men in ferocity.

The gases within the whales would have had their way,
Having increased within the carcasses, buoyant within the day,
Each floating to the surface, ready for harvest, waiting for tether,
But no move could be made upon them in this weather.

The water around Whale Spit Beach was like a kettle on the boil,
Far too dangerous for little boats, men so fragile, too large a toil,
The fortitude of men, so easily swayed by power of ocean or sea,
But that's the way it was, that is life, the way it will always be.

ORCINUS ORCA

By the fourth day it was accepted no more, and so with loud shout,
The boats forced themselves into the ferocity, heart's so stout,
The coast scoured both up and down for any sign of the whales,
But they had broken from the anchors, were lost amidst the gales.

And the torn looks upon the faces of the men told the story,
Gone were their wages, destroyed beyond regain, here no glory,
Drought scoured not only farmlands but ocean as well,
With it the optimism, panic striking hearts like ringing of bell.

Now was the time to face the reality of the situation,
George walked in on the men as they sat at their station,
The gloom around the table, cups of tea nestled in hand,
Sourly toasted the few choices they had, of where they did stand.

But the men refused to hear of it, banged at the top of table,
Refused to admit defeat, rallied to their captain's side most able,
To remain loyal, to be strong, to be steadfast in their conviction,
They would stay and continue, like men, to face their perdition.

Each was sure in mind that their fate was not written,
That there was plenty more on which to feed, that could be bitten,
They were sure as sure can be that the tide would turn to better,
That more whales were just around the corner awaiting fetter.

And as miraculous as it was, their words were correct,
Their harpoons and lances would not rust with neglect,
For they caught themselves two whales just two days later,
Nine in total over the next three weeks, each greeted by laughter.

SONG OF THE OCEAN

The conditioning, of both species, had sprung to life,
More than simple feelings, or gestures, came from this strife,
There was camaraderie amongst them, for each served the other,
Both men and Orcinus being... courteous, careful not to smother.

From the killers point of view the humans were nothing to adore,
Men were to be used to the best of their ability and nothing more,
And men understood that killers fell well to their duties,
Performed as desired and willed, an amalgamation of abilities.

Orcinus, competing for food: by such, escalating their abilities,
But also relying upon the energy and prowess of the other species,
But there was always room for improvement,
And plenty to learn and see, and great amazement.

To the men in boats it was part of the day, each working their roll,
Arduous work endured, but after time, like taking leisurely stroll,
For orca it was harvesting sustenance by means of collaboration,
The tethering of secular importance, and a great manipulation.

People and animals do all they can to secure a living, to survive,
Whether one receives money as reward, or a meal, each will strive,
It is of utmost importance, in life, to seek an opportunity,
To reap the rewards of harvest, of one's strenuous activity.

This was something that Tom knew well and put into practice,
He was no stranger, he was not simple, he was not novice,
He was more than adamant to learn and to influence,
To gain advancement and never be an inconvenience.

ORCINUS ORCA

The night was reasonably calm and flop-tailing called out,
A call to boats, for men to attend their duty, a loud shout,
One boat, faster than other, did disappoint Tom within the bay,
More boats the merrier: a faster kill, no time to delay.

George's crew flashed ahead of Alex Grieg's boat,
Separated by a football field of misery, but they did not gloat,
Such brought on a suffering misery for Alex that night,
One short lived for George, nothing there to cause great plight.

Suddenly a right whale showed itself by spouting high and wide,
Moon beams glistening off skin of monster, waves he did ride,
Followed by the disturbance of water, the bubbling of surface,
As killers bit with all their might, thrashing about at fast pace.

Arthur Ashby took his position with pride and hurled his harpoon,
Threw with all the power he could muster, not too late or soon,
It stuck, fast fish secure, and it then turned tail, of sturdy mind,
Commenced to head out to sea, trying to leave the boats behind.

The whale was secured, the rope let out, a good, tactical strike,
Although further away from the shore then they would like,
Not only this but Alex and his crew were falling further behind,
Spurring themselves on by power of oar, speed playing on mind.

Tom then saw the dilemma and acted immediately,
Pulled away from the fray, stripping the others of his ability,
Pod members looked upon him briefly and with anxiousness,
Opening their mouths, exposing their teeth, an aggressiveness.

SONG OF THE OCEAN

Noisily clapping their jaw together, voicing their anger,
Frustrated by Tom vacating his post, his audacity, his demeanour,
They displayed their dissatisfaction, their displeasure,
Tom's unpredictable act could lose them their treasure.

With sudden amazement, Tom grabbed onto the whale line,
Allowed himself to be pulled along, the act so hard to define,
The green boat just a dozen feet behind him as the whale slowed,
The men flabbergasted to say the least, Tom now being towed.

The very implication that Tom was helping, was sheer ludicrous,
But there it was; so absurd, hard to believe, so ridiculous,
Tom was slowing the progress of the whale to such a degree,
That Alex and crew were gaining ground: Tom, a legend to be.

It was painted clear as a picture for all to see,
The other crew catching up along their side, upon the lee,
And here the harpooner of the other boat stood, good stance,
Secured against concave of the thwart, towards whale did glance.

Alex let loose with the second harpoon for the day,
To secure a link, to remain fastened, lance to strike as they may,
Tom then released his hold upon the line and re-joined his pod,
Having gained much approval from all of the men with a nod.

Suddenly the space between the ribs was pierced by lance,
The death-throes of whale illuminating the killer's exuberance,
Forcing their way into the mouth of the dying whale at a flood,
Tearing at his lips as from the blowhole came much blood.

ORCINUS ORCA

The whale was putting up a hell of a fight,
At one stage leapt more than 16 feet into sight,
Seen with three killers still attached to his lip,
A vision to behold as he tried to flip.

The right whale was losing his energy for no reward,
Five more minutes and it's all over as boats surge forward,
The combined efforts of man and beast having won the day,
Life over for another mammal, so great was the fray.

With the whale was marked as usual, anchor and marker attached,
Dawned then upon George an opportunity, a new scheme hatched,
He looked over the men, gave orders, oars to ocean, to embrace,
As into the murky waters the killers, with meal, did race.

Orcinus would do as they pleased, in 24 hours George to return,
The humpback would re-float, ready to be towed, ready to churn,
George then announced of his moments thought and reflection,
To secure yesterday's kill early, drag her in, men called to action.

And fortune served the whalers, gases having completed their job,
Now ready to tow her back to try-works, 4.5 miles, no short lob,
But the night was pleasant: cold, the moon shone above,
The task most achievable, one to warm the core, not to love.

The markers were sought, pulled in and the anchor too,
Several ropes attached to the carcass, tied well as they knew,
And the men braced for the hard slog home, to work all night,
Heading for the coastal town, for their beacon, their light.

SONG OF THE OCEAN

Their backs broke under the strain,
But as they say, no pain, no gain,
And 4.5 miles was a big ask, a large price to render,
The tide a little against them, the moon watching in wonder.

In time the moon would make its way across the sky to the west,
Bringing a little relief in the form of medium tide at its best,
But that was far away at present, not to be seen anytime soon,
Currently of thought was a warm bed, after soup with a spoon.

Although the weather seemed to be in their favour,
Their previous task and this long haul was too much labour,
With little energy they pushed on, not superheroes of action,
But of flesh and bone, disciplined by money, the true motivation.

They pulled upon the oars with all their strength and might,
Continued on as best they could against the tide this night,
The lights ahead of them showed where Twofold Bay lay,
But it was still very far off, so very far away.

After hours of pulling the monster behind,
So little progress having assaulted the mind,
With hardened hands starting to show signs of wear,
Men over-worked, a heavy strain, fabric of souls did tear.

Another thirty minutes and George waved the white flag,
Their bones worn, bodies shot, exhausted, strips of rag,
They now head on home without the cargo hence tied,
To return in the morning, after good rest, sleep no longer denied.

ORCINUS ORCA

THE HEINOUS CRIME

In 1904 the number of killer whales was altered by one,
Unprecedented and unfortunate, to their cores it stung,
Before the eyes of most, including George, in boat, in bay,
With rudder in his palms, skies pleasant, open, and grey.

He was near where a whale had been buoyed and anchored,
Set upon entrance to bay where it had been stored,
Awaiting the gases to build, the bulge to move and re-float,
Any time now, dead whale to be seen, he cleared his throat.

And here it came, a gentle breaking, the surface disturbed,
No reasonable explanatory to employ, no decent word,
Ready for towing, to try-works to mend,
To deblubber in earnest, to cut and rend.

The try-works, men surrendering to work to be accursed,
Back-breaking at best and back-breaking at worst,
Suffering the intolerable smell and flies as they fly,
Seagulls on the light breeze, pestering beaks that defy.

One of the men in the boat was suddenly drawn to a chase,
Pointed it out to the others for cheer, not to abase,
For Jackson was alone, chasing a grampus over surf,
Gaining ground on the dolphin in violation of his turf.

SONG OF THE OCEAN

The dolphin's all-inspiring effort to escape its devastating future,
A bleak and unconditional devouring which was to be a butcher,
Men smiled as they watched the chase and pulled upon their oars,
Ready to give momentary shout, ready to give open applause.

Suddenly they were all filled with fright,
Anxiousness that lasted mere seconds upon the fight,
Continuing to look upon the scene so far away,
So wide and expansive was the bay.

Jackson, so well through the shallows he propelled, he steers,
Breaking waves, crystal clear, upon beach and amidst leers,
But the chase was about to meet its end as grampus moved aside,
And Jackson fell upon the sandy beach; high and dry, end of ride.

Only his flukes felt the stimulus and comfort of water upon him,
He thrashed about in an effort to free himself of situation so grim,
As the grampus made its way safely back towards the open ocean,
And the men seeing the dilemma, Jackson and his lack of motion.

Too far from the water's edge to secure delivery into the surf,
Unable to move himself back into that place of his birth,
Without the assistance of the men of Eden and their green boat,
He was doomed to die there, on the beach, never again to float.

Without further ado they steered towards the killer as he thrash,
Trying to regain ground upon retreating waves, in them to dash,
The moon high in the sky, upon the other side of the globe,
Pulling tide from beneath Jackson, as though from man a robe.

ORCINUS ORCA

The men felt that they had little time to procure a rescue,
Jackson would not function well upon the beach of hue,
And as they rowed, they saw, gulls make good of the opportunity,
Set on down and stand their ground, clear of harm's way in unity.

Gulls, looking upon the giant killer with eyes as large as saucers,
Squawking, stomachs to be filled, a gathering of scroungers,
Wishing with all their will to be able to peck out the drying eyes,
To take any advantage, to savour what they could with no ties.

And then a figure came into view as it walked Aslings Beach,
On towards Jackson, every step characteristic of body speech,
Harry Silks, homeless and obtuse, had seen the orca wash ashore,
With inward feelings so harshly felt, of orca he did deplore.

The men collaborated on Silks as he suddenly sprang into action,
He seeing George and men in their green boat, and their reaction,
Commenced to run fast towards Jackson, neither astute nor shy,
Seemingly wishing to be first upon the scene; but why?

The men continued upon their salvation of the killer whale,
Whom meant so much to them, of significance never to pale,
Silks acting suspiciously, without good cause or good reason,
Making ground fast upon orca, as though out to cause treason.

The whalers, wishing no more than to see Jackson safe from harm,
See him turned back into the surf, to aspire and calm that alarm,
The calming of inner terror, to impart their aid in this situation,
Unable to fathom the outcome to unfold: shaken from foundation.

SONG OF THE OCEAN

And in full view of crew Silks withdraw a knife from a scabbard,
    Stabbed the defenceless whale to death so very hard,
    Followed quickly by his running away, so fast he bolt,
    From the threats flung his way, of the verbal assault.

Several other orca had rallied to the scene of the splashing fluke ,
    Poor Jackson unable to effect good move, of ocean to rebuke,
They too struck hard by the horrific scene, no laughable banter,
An astounding and heart-breaking offence, of needless slaughter.

    And come what may, Tom and the others departed the bay,
        Shocked and exasperated, for a few days, away to stay,
    What would become of the contract between man and beast?
        What was to become of Silks? Something at least.

            Unknown to the killer whales of this town,
    Silks was escorted away, never to be of good renown,
        By the local law enforcers for his own protection,
    Never to be seen of again, to help relieve the tension.

George undertook to repair the damage done, began legal action,
    By first writing a letter to the Eden Progress Association,
    To have the orca protected by law, to have them conserved,
    To feel as though some form of justice had been served.

    And within a few days another humpback was steered,
        By fewer in number, fewer dorsal appeared,
    The devastation of Jackson's slaughter, his killing,
    Had seen the pods' number take a large milling.

ORCINUS ORCA

THE DEATH

August 1907: Stranger was killed by a fisherman in Botany Bay,
Mother to Tom and Hooky, of her absence men pray,
These two siblings of ocean and sea, so fond of Eden and shore,
Felt the bite of separation more than anything, though little rancor.

And it wasn't just the matter of fact that their mother had died,
Nor that their matriarch long, aspiring life had been denied,
But of sadness, that human intervention had failed them again,
Upon their cooperation, their friendship, a great pain and stain.

Their mother had been killed by a fisherman for no good reason,
Death sentence to fall, for procuring fish from a net, not treason,
No orca had ever murdered a man, never heard in all of history,
But man had deliberately killed many Orcinus, some for glory.

What ensured that a killer whale 'did not' take the life of a man?
Was it the sense that a human was intelligent, a mammal, of clan?
Why should intelligence procure sanctity and life?
Why did Orcinus refrain from delivering man that great strife?

Not surprising should it be that Tom and Hooky were then absent,
Did not appear in the bay for a year, of their anger to vent,
To return the next, bringing new invigoration,
To start afresh with a greater determination.

SONG OF THE OCEAN

But Cooper and Big Ben were more than just friends of Stranger,
Found the parting by death too much to bear, had too much anger,
And so they departed the bay almost immediately thereafter,
With their son Young Ben, though not Albert, their daughter.

Albert, their daughter, chose to remain behind, more to spore,
For she had mothered Charlie Adgery a few years before,
But others were in two minds as to whether to stay,
Or whether to follow the path of others and to stray.

Shortly after, further demise did strike the pod with bad news,
That Big Ben was dead, filling ocean with low-pitched mews,
Dying when stranded on the rocks at Leather Jacket Bay,
Young Ben returned alone, little solace secured, but not to stay.

It was a terrible year for the pod of killers of the bay,
Affecting them all in some small or large way,
First there was Jackson in 1904, and now Stranger,
Followed shortly after by Big Ben, always the eager.

Times were changing; vibrations and smells of ocean told the tale,
They were growing old, their minds seemingly weary and stale,
Vast reservoir of good memories evaporating, replaced by sad,
What was to become of them all? Were victories still to be had?

To the men, whaling was whaling, it mattered little,
Other than price they were to receive, of this resource so brittle,
Regardless of the amount of effort and time displaced,
Whether the whale was big or small it would still be embraced.

ORCINUS ORCA

Equipment was important, boats best of all they did possess,
If a catch could be secured for little outlay as possible, little stress,
With no damage dealt upon the boats, then it was a good catch,
And one worth remembering on which memory could latch.

But one of the most recalled will be little reflected on by history,
Though a record of the grandest proportion exists, of this story,
Will never be excelled hereafter, for bay whaling is no longer,
And that was in 1910, its capture, a 98 foot blue, if not larger.

The sheer size made the catch a momentous occasion,
For those at the oars were in sheer awe and placation,
But it wasn't so much a case of capture, than one of surrender,
And so we shall extravagate a little of this monstrous stranger.

The blue had a calf that measured over half the mother's length,
A monster which totalled around 98 tonnes: muscle, fat, strength,
Enough oil and bone to tear the stitches of any money bag,
Regardless of form and manufacture, purse to wave the white flag.

The call of RUSHO! went out firm and loud as in the past,
The panting of horse from lookout and flop-tailing to last,
Boast manned, waters entered, ready to secure a humpback,
What they met was sheer disbelief, a blue, and size it did not lack.

By the time they were positioned, ready to deliver their prowess,
George sitting, shoulders back, to harpoon silently bless,
The killers had hounded the mother to such a desperate level,
She did breach upon the shore, great size on which to marvel.

SONG OF THE OCEAN

Orcinus had performed so well that the blue was out of reach,
For them no lip and tongue, but the calf was far from beach,
It was the least exciting of all the catches they could remember,
Though so easy for the men, like draining water from manger.

The band of just six killers had done their job well,
A small group compared to before, each year their numbers fell,
Now further on, up the coast, close knit and in rank strung,
Not altogether displeased with the capture of the young.

It was a formidable task, that blue whale so large, no boast,
It could have taken much time to capture if further from coast,
Without the jagged shore the killers alone could not have won,
Not over this whale [she would be lost] weighing so many tonne.

There was still that exuberance from Humpy's pod, all pleased,
Pleasure that surged through them, pleasure which they released,
By show-boating and larking about, jumping from the ocean,
Breaching here and there upon surface, their home and station.

A trophy to be remembered amongst old saddle patches and new,
Remembered by Kinscher, Little Jack, and Big Jack as they grew,
And here they celebrated, showing off their skills and acrobatics,
Lessons taught to the young, handed down, their excessive antics.

But what of Tom; what made him so different?
What was it that drove his ambition, it so apparent?
What reinforced his strong, unequivocal tolerance?
Why did he display an allegiance to man at first glance?

ORCINUS ORCA

Tom was a pioneer, a one and only in essence,
A creature bound by the fruits of intelligence,
Intelligence which left the others of his species far behind,
Of this situation... position... predicament: of different mind.

He understood, [a freak of nature], of mind most level,
like the lions, Ghost and the Darkness, but not evil,
Tom beheld unequalled knowledge, instincts of deliberation,
The lions devoured man through superior cunning and ambition.

Tom was a powerhouse of ability and procurement,
A wealth of interpretation within his head at the moment,
He was there to pave the way to the bright light of bonding,
Bonding even Darwin failed to see in the bloom of his bidding.

Tom was similar to man; he could feel hurt and embarrassment,
Feared death and displayed great courage, lived for the moment,
He, the ability to see beyond the makeup upon a man's exterior,
As an astronomer sees beyond the makeup of all that is superior.

SONG OF THE OCEAN

THE LOSS

Jimmy fought well on this day [31 years since birth], so snappy,
He came to Twofold Bay several years after the return of Humpy,
A time of upheaval when some killers departed and others stray,
A time of prosperity, of minor issues, a structure in decay.

Little did it matter under the sway of Stranger in years past,
Who for her years and with the power bestowed was sure to last,
Who stood as a strong matriarch with a long list of signals,
Many attack manoeuvres accredited her name, unwritten annuals.

Being far less boisterous than Tom, Jimmy was a quiet mammal,
Was mated with Big Jack, a female of ambition, a strong animal,
Her mother and father being 'offshore' variants, living off fish,
Particularly salmon, than anything else, the perfect dish.

Tired of their life and position in large pod they decided to stray,
Had opted for habitual change, found their way to Twofold Bay,
Here they stayed for several years before moving on once more,
Jimmy, enjoying life with mate Big Jack, stayed on, close to shore.

Big Jack had mothered Kinscher and Little Jack,
A female and a male, neither courage nor beauty did they lack,
Over the year, Jimmy's persona had grown quite substantially,
Amidst this pod of 15, not large or small, maintaining good tally.

ORCINUS ORCA

And this persona was not just from performance,
Not due to mistaken glance, or by pure chance,
Not because of any great feats noteworthy of praise or acclaim,
But since 1907 Big Jack had been matriarch, by name and fame.

Jimmy felt honoured, was of good position, suffered no neglect,
All brought on a blossom of change regards to effort and effect,
Such effort was accepted well by the other members of the pod,
Treated him well, always content to give him a friendly nod.

And there came a day when a humpback had been cornered,
Again their familiar assaults upon whale, all truly mastered,
Much effort sourced into tiring out this great beast so large,
To create that stress, horror, feeling of doom to hence discharge.

Again and again the blowhole was covered, humpback writhing,
Orca after orca thrown in order to impede its breathing,
Preventing the whale from sounding, to make for vast open water,
To escape through gate of Twofold Bay, to avoid the slaughter.

The men too, were present upon the surface of the ocean so wide,
Prodding away with their sticks of iron, over surface they glide,
Shifting positions, handling oars, yelling out above the noise,
Above the noise of war, to bring the whale to heel with poise.

Several harpoons had been thrown and one was not well secured,
The second had done its job well, lancing now assured,
Humpback putting up a good fight when Jimmy made his move,
To suffocate once and for all, then rip at its flank, nought to prove.

SONG OF THE OCEAN

And then something went horribly wrong, a blunt conclusion,
With so many lines in the water and so much confusion,
Such a melee, much flourish about the scene so hastily stack,
Jimmy become entwined with line and sank with the humpback.

The other killers assisted the humpback to the bottom of the bay,
Unaware of Jimmy's predicament, of his position, his last day,
Even the men failed to see anything amiss,
And then Jimmy was heard to cry out, shattering the bliss.

Suddenly Kinscher and Little Jack were alerted to the situation,
Jimmy unable to break free of the mess, now drew much attention,
So little could they do: Jimmy died there, so lovingly prod,
Amidst Kinscher, Little Jack, Big Jack, and others of the pod.

And so several of the pod fell to the pressures of the loss,
Big Jack soon departed, it was too much, now no longer the boss,
Walker [son of Humpy] following in her wake,
And now Young Ben departed for good, to his core it did shake.

For Young Ben the loss of his friend weighed too much on mind,
There had been too much death in the past, nothing left to bind,
Last but not least the following turned their fluke and swam away,
Albert, Skinner and Little Jack, for deeper waters to stay.

The following day the carcass was retrieved by George and crew,
Utterly astounded by what they found as nearer they drew,
To the scene of the floating carcass with Jimmy attached,
Buoyed and anchored with humpback, upon their minds so etched.

ORCINUS ORCA

A sorry sight, Jimmy strapped to its side, so secure and sound,
Like a baby strapped to its mother back, tightly bound,
A scene never seen before, a sheer jolt to the crew,
They cut the line away, allowing Jimmy to float from view.

Reminded they were, Humpy caught in lines of his making,
Though more fortunate for being noticed prior to whale sinking,
Humpy cut from the lines and set free before death,
Gifted chance at life, awarded another day, another breath.

The men remembered this day as the tragedy it was,
As too did the killer whales of the ocean, these grand orcas,
The whalers cut memory into the woodwork of Boyd Tower,
Along with Peter Lia, Jimmy to be remembered forever.

SONG OF THE OCEAN

THE TIME TO FORGET, THE TIME TO RECALL

The Norwegians, in 1913, had mustered 9,500 barrels of oil,
From the east coast of Australia, from its waters, not soil,
Not to dally long, the last of their chasers, to tomb to lay,
In comparison to other companies; a small amount during stay.

But the damage was done and the killer whale was made vacant,
From the waters of Eden, for great stints of time, this instant,
Then a dorsal did appear, through gentle surf, a gift from grave,
Accompanied by smiling faces, of those who knew, giving wave.

Tom was back with Sharkey, Youngster, Humpy,
Kinscher, Brierly, Charlie Adgery and Hooky,
Now the cooperation, of beast and man, continued as per the past,
With reflection upon old times coming clear, but would it last?

Reflections of securing 'fast fish', that joining of destinies,
Reflections upon the unwritten laws between the two species,
Reflections upon the slaughter, feeding on lips and tongue,
Reflections of fun, men receiving their money and victories won.

Other killers came and went over the years,
Although few in number, when parted, always tears,
And migrating whales were killed as they had always been,
Amidst this effort, a legendary corroboration as never before seen.

ORCINUS ORCA

By no surprise, Tom and George forgot the past: or did not know,
A time when laws sown [lips and tongue] took flower: to grow,
Each law opening a new beginning, the founding of friendship,
But the end was near, killers so few, in sight an end to kinship.

The most horrid of circumstance to hit, was the death of Sharkey,
Jackson's partner, a clash with the Norwegians most deadly,
Killed whilst feeding upon offerings of the ocean, now unclean,
Great Orcinus, the Norwegians so proud to sour and demean.

The Norwegians saw the killers as a pest and little more,
Little else mattered but filling the belly of ship with vast store,
And so Sharkey bought the brunt of their overzealous anger,
Brierly and Youngster then departed the bay of horrors for ever.

There was no bitterness towards those with whom they worked,
They were old and tired, less reliant, and mentally borked,
The whaling industry was faltering as orca numbers diminished,
Fewer each year returned to bloody grounds, they were finished.

WWII came, men disappeared, and once over, back to the ropes,
So many years away, hence their return saw many dashed hopes,
So few killers here now, new season, and a few new men to train,
Boats manned by casuals [not of iron] but unafraid of the rain.

Spring came and went and then summer, autumn and winter,
The same game played each year, mostly sweet, not bitter,
On some occasion there were three killers, at others five,
And the aggressive nature of orca: always heightened and alive.

SONG OF THE OCEAN

Even though individuals slowed a little in their old age,
Tom always felt young: of history he alone did turn the page,
In 1923 Kinscher and Charlie Adgery departed, in clear view,
And as the pod decreased in size, George's own family grew.

George, as per Tom, in all comparison to his colleague of ocean,
Remained as fearless as always, as though by some compulsion,
They were peas in a pod, one and the same, dogs of different tail,
A strong bond struck between the two, never weak, never frail.

Never before in the history, save rumours of a man and jungle,
Had man and beast [wolves] performed so well, to truly mingle,
Such performance you would swear had been orchestrated well,
But no, familiarity and trust made them unique, not magical spell.

We recall how in the early twenties, the anchor rope, the painter,
How Tom would quite often grab it so men did not saunter,
It being thrown to him, how he did tow the boat towards whale,
To make good way, good speed upon humpback like strong gale.

Sometimes speedily overtaking George's opposition,
Those that prey on same target, upon them a deflation,
Holding dearly onto the 60 fathoms of 2 inch coir rope, so keen,
Hence preventing others gaining ground, before those of green.

Tom did this in order to secure the kill, to stay alive,
He, and pod, needed the sustenance in order to survive,
Without the aid of George, Tom would meet his end all the sooner,
Without Tom's aid, the green boats would have been the loser.

ORCINUS ORCA

Jackie Warren did witnessed the phenomena known as Tom,
In 1926 saw him grab the line of boat, to take it from,
And towed along the surface of ocean so longing and pure,
For the purpose of enjoyment, not for whale to catch or lure.

Or Margaret Brooks having her breath taken by such antics,
Tom pulling against the 'White Heather', of his heroics,
Tugging hard on tow rope, to prevent him taking the prize,
Seemingly depriving the orca, beast of ocean and sea so wise.

Yes indeed, they were times to remember, never to forget,
Times that saw little evaluation by historians which we'll regret,
Soon, however, there was only Tom and two others that remain,
Most having taken to different waters, for their meals to gain.

Neither joining super pods nor really deviating from them,
But remaining unto themselves, too old to grow new stem,
Yet some young members did bud new matrilineal linkage,
And some died, either peaceably or in fights most savage.

It seemed to Tom that his entire life had been spent with men,
His home at Twofold Bay, a history of its own to pen,
Two species having come together in times of hardship and need,
Whether bonding for years, or decades, they finally agreed.

As for Tom's family; well, he had little to show for his merits,
For his offspring had separated from him as nature permits,
Their mother, Tom's mate, refusing to leave her pod of transients,
Tom, never truly feeling alone, discouraging was life's variants.

SONG OF THE OCEAN

And year after year saw fewer whales secured for savoury meal,
Orcinus forced to pursue other means of nourishment most real,
To other hunting grounds that did prove fruitful for their needs,
To the great disappointment of old friends and their creeds.

ORCINUS ORCA

THE MIRACULOUS FIND AND SAD FALL

So many years behind him and so many deaths to date,
George, so ever thankful, that most experiences were first rate,
Each vastly good and few instances of horror and devastation,
But old memories die and new fill the void, no deliberation.

George, married, had a son by the name of Jack, one of three,
And this a recollection of how Tom gave him a dose of dignity,
Handing back to him, his friend so close, in need and desire,
In the year of our Lord, 1926, a miraculous saving, one to admire.

There came a day where the small family of five plus relatives,
Met tragedy, their dinghy submerged, weather endangering lives,
The three children gone missing not more than a dozen feet away,
Freak storm, no warning, a search well needed, on much to pray.

It was a sad fact of fate that saw three deaths in one day,
In a storm which lashed out its evil in more than one way,
The fact of the case is as basic as one, two, three,
A most depressing engagement worth cancelling with glee.

But now married to the fate so devilish flung,
George and family did all they could, no herald sung,
And if Tom were there at the time of the heinous storm,
He would have aided them all, with truth shall hearts warm.

SONG OF THE OCEAN

This he proved over the days by entering Bay and approaching,
Closing upon the scene, many boats searching for the missing,
Searching frantically for the bodies of the three that were torn,
Taken from mother most cherished, age now hauntingly worn.

The first two children were found soon enough:
The girl pulled deceased from shallow waters once rough,
And a boy's body from the sandy bottom, his legs most visible,
As for Jack, nothing was found, and all remained most miserable.

Tom could see something amiss, but didn't understand what,
The men were searching for something, upon the area they squat,
Combing over the sea floor, time and time again in their boats,
Grappling hooks out, looking for sign, wrapped in warm coats.

Tom then bombarded the area with his skills taken for granted,
The signals received forming clear picture, he was so astounded,
He could see the body of Jack beneath the surface without fail,
Just beneath the sand where the boats had searched to no avail.

Over the next few days, after the weather beautiful and serine,
Tom continued up and down Whale Spit, hoping to be seen,
Trying with all his presence to show the world what he knew,
He had found the remains of the one the weather cast and threw.

George looked upon his friend of the sea with great admiration,
Tom's presence in his time of need, a mark of respect, a lavation,
For it suddenly dawned that Tom might have something to say,
Was here as a friend most dear to lift the lid on the days so grey.

ORCINUS ORCA

Tom could see the expression upon George's face,
The sparkle of wonder in his eyes, a reflection of grace,
The methodical ticking away of the brain within his head,
The mind of a man whom is not that easily read.

Tom could see that George had realised the antics of energy spent,
Called for the boat to do another sweep where Tom lay persistent,
And soon found Jack beneath the sand, drew him upon the shore,
Tom followed the boat, paying his respects and very much more.

The other two were buried just two days before sibling Jack,
Now he, bestowed unto hallowed ground, of compassion no lack,
Forty cars, more; vast number having respects to lay, much to say,
Following the hearse as it drew into the cemetery opposite the bay.

Such a large congregation of people: great assembly, great lot,
All in complete silence, many in black, there on the spot,
Only the soft tones of the priest lifting themselves to the breeze,
Floating down towards the bay, no clear understanding to seize.

Tom had completed his duty well, a right hand man, a deputy,
Had offered assistance to his friend, beyond the call of duty,
The bond so strong between, one that could never be broken,
Above and beyond the law of the tongue, so openly spoken.

Such bond between them both was what made Tom so strong,
Despite many situations that had turned out to be so wrong,
It was doubtful that Tom would have lived as long as his did,
If not for the law which saw this tether, so secure and splendid.

SONG OF THE OCEAN

The men had served him well, as he served them, from so young,
Not just a one-way ticket of servitude for taste of lip and tongue,
And the very sustenance that it offered was beyond all compare,
What they did with a whale's body after death, what did he care.

But the service he had paid this man of men was not forgotten,
And so, after the burial service George did attend, so here written,
George did pay visit to the shore; not to pay respects to children,
But to say a heart-felt thankyou to his true friend of the ocean.

It was then that Tom turned into the bay and made his way,
With the remainder of his pod to head off a humpback stray,
One with calf, allowing themselves to be caught unawares,
A fight with the Orcinus and his most awesome of stares.

He turned and thrust his flukes, through the water so fast,
Slicing through the waters of the bay, to join the fray at last,
Joining in on the waiting struggle which simply had to be won,
For they had not fed for quite some time, hence not here for fun.

And as George had lost his children to the ever waking ocean,
Tom too, lost a friend this year, to the calling of waves in motion,
For Hooky, son of Stranger, fathered by a stray,
Recognised by dorsal so bent, left forever the bay.

It was time to face the facts as they were staged before them all,
The crew was made up mostly of new, broad, short and tall,
They seemed inexperienced, inept, when compared to years past,
At a time before the war, which took the men away, fodder so cast.

ORCINUS ORCA

The single boat now manned by crew, faces ever changing,
The ocean gifting fewer opportunities, all less engaging,
Orcinus orca growing old and weary, call made for substitute,
A move to easier quarry, less palatable, less astute.

Killers whales on the move,
Manned crews losing the grove,
Bay whaling changing as an industry,
The drawing of curtain upon ancestry.

But the men who served here would recall Humpy and Tom,
Frolicking freely in the bay, not knowing where they were from,
Having been here since a very young age,
To become a memory in history, written upon page.

And the two killers were not as agile as they once were,
Breaching the waters with less… ambition, but still sincere,
A stranger passing may think how free-spirited they appeared,
Watching them play, awake to the world, but somehow feared.

For the orca, no care in the world: they were aptly… longevous,
To bystanders who knew no difference, young and mischievous,
But George… he knew the truth, could picture it all, understood,
They were old, short in tooth, age to betray them all, for good.

1927 and the pod of two seemed to be of little worse for wear,
Once a pod of fifty more, strong in virtue, but no longer there,
A vast repertoire of song to corral humpbacks with great ease,
Allowing them to coral and secure a meal, one to please.

SONG OF THE OCEAN

Humpy: older than Tom and frailer by action and thought,
Partnered with Typee, mother to Walker, so lovingly sought,
Knew of Jackson's death, by the hand of Silks: a demented mind,
But orca do not convey ideas in patterned speech like mankind.

She had once led attack after attack upon whales of all size,
Had ripped chunks from their lips and flank to gain her prize,
Had once become entangled in line and freed by George,
A conviction of mind therefore cast in gold, friendship to forge.

Humpy lead a pod until 1880, prior to temporary departure,
In 1885 was next in line for position of matriarch, to nurture,
Yes indeed, a great history, a story to be told, many memories,
But Humpy's days were almost over, so too the many glories.

They heard a humpback some miles out, followed in her wake,
Contemplating their next strategic move, much at stake,
A move without the aid of man, one that they would regret,
Like any other attack, apart from their number, therefore a threat.

They took chunk after chunk, pressing home the stress and fear,
So overwhelming, bitter-sweet aggression, a double-ended spear,
And so it is here that Humpy received a wound to the face,
An eye lost in the fight, inflicted upon her abilities: no disgrace.

The whale made its escape as Tom came in close to his friend,
A friend no-closer could he have been, right to the very end,
They fed on the whale, but this would not last them long,
Soon upon them both would be herald the end of the song.

ORCINUS ORCA

The line had now been drawn for Humpy to see,
Within the week she was dead, gone her hunting ability,
Tom left to hunt food on his own, though no longer willing,
Maybe a small calf if able, but life was over, no longer thrilling.

SONG OF THE OCEAN

THE DEPARTED

And so now there was just Tom, all alone,
A good life, having nothing for which to atone,
Dying on 16th September, 1930, shy of midnight,
The end of a legend in his own right.

A week before his death he had put chase to a grampus dolphin,
Taking chunks from the mammal until it died: a victory, a win,
It was a fairly quick death, a short fight,
It took a lot out of Old Tom, his last meal, his last bite.

The grampus was a meal, a king's ransom, not to be forgotten,
A great treat for an old warhorse, the blubber sweet, not rotten,
Lips and tongue taken great advantage of, better than most,
The fight seen by small crowd onshore, a splendid scene to toast.

And it dawned upon all those of Twofold Bay,
That Old Tom was alone, to eat and to play,
Not another killer to be seen anywhere about,
All quiet and bare, as far as the wind could carry a shout.

A week later and he was found dead,
After a day of frolicking, good life lead,
Flop-tailing into the breeze, on a day so bright,
And with the setting of the sun he said his good night.

ORCINUS ORCA

His teeth bared the brunt of his years, now the worst of his flaws,
More worn in areas where he had taken the painter in his jaws,
His efforts to assist the men in their green boats now proved,
To be a devastating blow to his life, a life now removed.

Yes indeed, Tom had remained loyal to the end,
To all of those he had come to know, a great friend,
More knew of him than he could possibly know of them,
And that is where the tale does end and legend does stem.

Yes indeed, he enjoyed those last hours in this place,
Showing himself temporarily upon the surface with grace,
Onlookers thinking that something was amiss,
The next day his body floated into Snug Cove, gone the bliss.

Tom, recognised without mistake, his distinctive dorsal, his mast,
A fin which had been photographed so many times in the past,
A dorsal caught on camera in 1910, to forever last,
He died, simply, from old age, lived a life so full, so vast.

It was now, as his body lay still upon the beach,
That his genitalia proved once and for all, a lesson to teach,
That he was in fact a male, a long history so grand,
How had he managed near 80 years, so hard to understand.

J.R.Logan funded suggestion that preservation was the key,
For Tom's story to remain alive and well, for eternity,
And a suggestion saw to it that his skeleton was provided a home,
A museum built, history shielded as though beneath a dome.

SONG OF THE OCEAN

The Eden Killer Whale Museum still exists today,
Puts the mind into a spin of all that visit the bay,
Over the tales that can be told or simply uncovered,
Of Tom, all in one place, history on plate so offered.

No one can deny the truth, for the truth is documented so well,
Tom was a male orca, 22 feet long, of abilities much to tell,
With a dorsal fin of 5.6 feet high,
Nothing of this fine specimen can anyone deny.

Tom was gone and bay whaling had come to an end,
In 1932 George hung up his harpoon, end of era, end of trend,
The crew disbanded to secure work in other fields,
To discover new sources of income, to discover new yields.

A few orca came back from time to time, memories to deliver,
Laying visit to the bay, upon the mouth of the Towamba River,
But these visits saw little action being carried out,
No humpback tackled, no prey, no "RUSHO" to shout.

The tide was changing across the entire country, so quick, so fast,
Whaling across the country was dying, from culture it was blast,
And it is strange to understand from the human point of view,
How the orca could alter human tactics, tactics of the hunt renew.

The orca were adverse, could make miracles from nature,
Saw change and hence relocated to other grounds, more rapture,
Understanding that their easy feeding was over with in the bay,
And so sought new choice, meals from new place of stay.

ORCINUS ORCA

But even now as the darkness continues to fall over George,
Contemplating the life of the pods during the years they forge,
Of their presence and their interaction with the Yuin years before,
That maybe the killer whale will return to Eden, ever more.

Humpback whales frequent the bay and splash around in play,
Their calves by their sides enjoy the warmth of water in bay,
To relax and feed with little concern or danger from attack,
George and other men watching, to older times taken back.

And today, from the darkness of time comes a reminder of past,
For even now Orcinus can be seen near Eden, water so vast,
Where the picturesque port town and with its ocean views,
Continue to provide delight to passers-by, not whaling crews.

Now science is on the killer's side, to confirm, quite adamantly,
That they are intelligent creatures, naturally and mentally,
With acoustic senses, social coordination, and self-awareness,
Learn rapidly, are innovative, a sheer delight, nothing less.

SONG OF THE OCEAN

THE END IS NIGH, TIME TO SAY GOODBYE

To an Orca, in general, the human race is a hindrance,
His desire and greed for commercial blubber his romance,
As he continued, without breath, to exploit the oceans and seas,
To settle those whims for oil, to do unto the species as he please.

Upon all countries of the world, in particular if coast does exist,
To turn the seas and oceans into paddocks and treat with iron fist,
To the Antarctic and Arctic, no measure, no explicit limit,
Where there was whale, there was oil, his credit, his permit.

And unbeknown to the orca of Twofold Bay, these killers of Eden,
In 1945 the International Whaling Conference, a whales warden,
Prepared extensive regulations for the part-protection of species,
To serve all whales as never before, to them great mercies.

This followed in 1946 by the International Whaling Commission,
Drawing conclusion that laws be adhered, without omission,
For international regulations should be put into place,
For these measures, henceforth, be maintained with grace.

Not simple conservation of the whales themselves,
But the stock levels of species so drawn from shelves,
And in 1949 a solar gathering of members did come together,
To maintaining principle and projects for protection, not to dither.

ORCINUS ORCA

In particular of the females,
The calves and young whales,
Sanctuaries and limitations on the number of kills,
To offer a sacred number, limit how much blood men spills.

The lowering of numbers has since slowed but not ceased,
A stranglehold on killings did seem to be released,
Possibly good reason why Orcinus changed routines,
Deviating from routes, upon places it so frequently leans.

But in the case of Twofold Bay was a special case, one alone,
Where men and killer aided the other, reaping blubber from bone,
And it was the men who aided the killer whale,
The killer exploited man, not such a far-fetched tale.

Twofold Bay offered much to Orcinus orca, its potential seen,
Not only was it a natural corral for which to entrap baleen,
But it was shallow enough to restrict a whale's escape,
Its position alone migration routes and its general shape.

Leather Jacket Bay was also a natural wonder,
Employed well by the killers, this place from down-under,
For the season of whaling suited their endeavours, much to reap,
The pleasant currents permitting a leisurely pace, awake or asleep.

It was all a matter of strategy to the killer whale,
They chose the ground upon which to feed, with little fail,
Where such was to take place and the method to be employed,
By which means death was to be inflicted, a whale best annoyed.

SONG OF THE OCEAN

And by 1952 George Davidson is dead,
Such a splendid bay life he had lead,
He was not alone in death, loved ones aside, Tom in head,
As Tom had died, alone beneath the ocean wave, so laid to bed.

The relationship between the two will live on forever,
A slice of history, Australia should be proud with fever,
Not for the relationship between these two different species,
But the acts of love, the affection shared, for all of their mercies.

If we look deep enough we can see how the men under George,
Gave up much, to work effectively with the orca, magic to forge,
Their equipment and techniques were of the old school,
Their foresight, courage and wit, not from any old fool.

These were not greedy men and nor were they wicked or cruel,
They had a job to do and did it well, the ocean their sacred tool,
But the men did believe they manipulating the killer whale,
Against all incursion, to prevail [Maybe you're doing it now].

How is it that a killer whale can put behind it the nature of the sea,
The nature of his species; the torments of their world that be,
That they can befriend man for gain, and all significance fades,
Learnt to work with man, maintain relationship for many decades.

If all killer whales were the same then should we assume,
That there be more of this cooperation, for growth more room,
Or are we drawn to a reality whereby this is one killer alone,
Made good a situation to suit the needs of matriarch upon throne.

ORCINUS ORCA

The name Tom should be celebrated, for he was a one and only,
And if there is never another then the world would be lonely,
For we, as human beings, need these experiences in our lives,
Instil a greater commodity than killing, an ambition that thrives.

Maybe the future will behold another just like him,
If not then it is possible that life will be grim,
For George, possibly, the last memories that drift from his mind,
Tom: a friend who could never be forgotten, one so hard to find.

SONG OF THE OCEAN

THE HISTORY

1712

It was in 1712 that the first of the sperm whale was taken from the safe harbour of its home in the sea near Nantucket, far from the waters of the Australian coast, but where several ancestors of those in the Eden pod had once frequented. The oil was considered much more valuable than that harvested by the bay whalers [shore fishing which had been a development of the Red Indians in similarity, but not a union as that of the Yuin of Twofold Bay]. Deep sea whaling was now an investment anxiously pursued; the curtain had been raised and the slaughter begun; an infringement upon the Orca's right to feed on all that swam in any of the oceans or seas.

1788

The settlement of Australia takes hold at the same time that the South Pacific is exploited for what it holds within its parlour of delights, 1,800 souls shipped to Botany Bay and they too, commence fishing within its waters.

ORCINUS ORCA

1790s

By the 1790s sperm whale fishing had spread to more favourable grounds, where they were seen to be in such large numbers that the opportunity could not be refused, hence the decimation of the South Pacific did commence, and although the killer whale tended to lay more towards the coastlines of many countries for their sustenance, routes across the great expanses of sea were patrolled.

1791

Many shoals were seen by members of the ship Britannia, from Van Diemen's Land to just out from the coast of Port Jackson, at approximately nine miles, and the numerous sightings were recorded for the prosperity of the captain but divulged, in the end, to the governor for the Australian people and its fishing industry. The endeavours and efforts, therefore, of the human race helped dictate, within reasonable terms, that the killers should direct their attentions more favourably to the coastline where migratory routes of humpback were known to exist.

Within a few short years of this sighting another was recorded to the west of the Galapagos Islands where sperm whales were seen in large quantities, copulation a common occurrence. It was now a basis of knowledge, something known by the killers for centuries, that one particular migratory route led along the coast of East Australia and out towards the islands so famous of Darwin and his findings. Not only this but the waters of the Pacific, to the north-east of New Zealand, were bountiful with sperm whales and their off-spring, so much so that the vast area, too large to contemplate, was combed by ships of many nationalities including those from Australia.

1799

Matthew Flinders stood upon the deck and saw that Twofold Bay could easily make a grand harbour, the skeleton of a right whale visible on the beach. A thought then traversed his mind where he was reminded of the days of Captain Cook, where he very nearly entered the east coast of Australia at the point where Twofold Bay opened itself to the world, but due to bad weather was forced to the north where Botany Bay was chosen for the first settlement.

1804

It wasn't long before the commercial value of whaling hit the minds of those that continued to colonize Tasmania, where right whales [sometimes referred to as black whales] frequented the bays with their calves from June to October. This provided great opportunity to hunt sperm whale during the summer months and then the bay whales in winter, through the exuberance of those that lanced the whales till their heart's content, fell upon the realization that hunting from row boats was as good, if not better, than ramming home their harvest from large ships; bay whaling was now a true profession and taken up by a few bays along the coast of Australia where migratory whales tempted the greed and thirst of human desire for oil.

Sites were selected with great care as many considerations needed to take point, namely shelters for the men, cookhouse, cooperage [where casks and barrels of all description could be made and repaired, to be filled to the brim with that marvellous substance], storehouses and try-works where slabs of blubber could be easily drawn up a ramp and prepared for boiling, extracting the gold so laboriously sought.

1828

It soon became an interest, the Yuin and their exploits, and Twofold Bay made the headlines in a Sydney newspaper, bay whaling adopted soon after as more of an experiment than anything else. The spoils were so great that the opportunity could not be ignored. It was shortly after that 16 white men of a dispatch from Sydney were killed and another five years elapsed before Dr.A.Imlay secured over a thousand acres of land in the area.

The indigenous people of the region around Twofold Bay are called Yuin and had a name for the killers; they called them 'Beowas', meaning brothers or kin, they were 'transient, a social organization of killer whale which was set aside from the 'resident' and 'offshore', but with many 'resident' characteristics; they were, in essence, a 'matrilineal' organisation of killers that were, to a degree, inseparable.

As per the Romans and Greeks before them, the Aboriginals of Australia looked upon the killer whales with great respect and admiration, believing wholeheartedly that they were the reincarnation of ancestors past, where the dead took the form of a wolf of the sea. Why?

The Yuin believed that the killer whales were the returned spirits of the dead, ancestors that had come back to the world of the living and to help provide sustenance to the indigenous population. If a monster of the deep was to provide such great amounts of food for the tribe then it must be nothing less than the reincarnated spirit of a recently deceased member for their society. They were, every one, treasured as original members of the tribe and known, not only to help feed the Yuin, but also to protect them whilst in the water.

For long before the presence of any white man, the Yuin – not exploiting – made good advantage of the situation where it was quite common for baleen whales to be herded into the bay and become stranded upon the beach, whereby the strategies of the hunt become a symbolised benefit to all in the tribe and the 'Beowas' were adopted into their beliefs. It was a phenomenon that could only be explained by the belief of the 'Beowas', for why else would a killer whale home in on a humpback caught in the bay, pester and kill, to feed upon the lips and tongue, and then allow all that which remained to be shored upon the beach in order for the Yuin to feed?

Much else was also sought by the Yuin, not just food and comradeship with a whale, but the more in-depth spiritual healing of infliction. It is here that rituals came into existence and all that the killer gave in jester to the people was to be used to full effect.

ORCINUS ORCA

A remedy evolved, where an individual so inflicted with rheumatism and the like would climb into a rotting carcase, naked and up to the neck in blubber, to gain the such sought-after relief gained by spending hours encased within the flesh and absorbing the stench and oil of the baleen's blubber.

1828 – 1830s

Thomas Raine was the first whaler in Twofold Bay in 1828, followed soon after in the 30's by the Imlay Brothers who employed several of the Yuin due to their keen ability to work hard, be reliable, and were easily skilled with the abilities of boat-handling; they were soon recognised for their talent and had good eyesight.

1838

Having sent for his brothers, Dr.Imlay undertook further exploits whereby his interest in breeding cattle continued alongside bay whaling.

1840

At this time the sperm whale industry took precedence for the humpback whale had become increasingly unavailable, learning over time to avoid the slaughter that occupied the bays of Tasmania, and although migratory routes were seldom changed and little voiced, it was in the interest of man to hunt where the value of the spoils could be secured in purse, hence the move from one species to the next; although, in all fair response, the sperm whale was also worth more in regards to oil.

1840s

In the 1840s, Benjamin Boyd set upon the scene and commenced to build a town in his own name; Boyd Town. It was his hope to have it grow in all aspects to one day be as big as any other city within Australia. He built a lighthouse from Sydney sandstone on the south head [Boyd Tower] along with a little church of red brick [the spire of which could be seen from 20 miles out to sea], houses, storage rooms, wharves, stock-yards and the Seashore Inn which is situated on the beach and draws upon the very romance of the area, all surrounded by the lushness of eucalyptus trees.

The bush itself was thick and descended to right upon the beach itself. Bay whaling was, however, not something that Boyd took too with great enthusiasm as the competition was so great, so sought to make an ambition from offshore whaling where the sperm whale could still be quarried in large numbers out to sea – for the sperm whale did not frequent the bays or the coast.

His crews were not successful, apparently bribed by the Imlay Brothers to miss-judge the thrust of a harpoon, but the oil from the sperm whale measured Boyd greed and filled him to the brim, his ships much more capable of bringing home the oil.

Oswald Briefly, a good friend of Boyd, who had arrived with him upon his yacht, Wanderer, made many written entries within a

ORCINUS ORCA

diary along with paintings and sketches of the activities of men and killer whales alike. It is from these accounts that the first encounter with the killers of Twofold Bay can be found, actually competing against the bay whalers as opposed to helping them, for the crews of bay refused to allow the killers a share and frequently attacked them with the boat spades used in removing blubber from the much sought after baleen. It is here that the first of many strange incidents commences to take shape for the killers begin to show a liking towards those crews less callous in their treatment towards them.

And the men of the crews that fought the whales from upon their long and sturdy craft took little pity on the killers for their help in the hunt. The men watch as the killer whales flung themselves upon the back of the whale, charging in and taking chunks from its flanks, pestering it at every turn in order to prevent it from careering home into the depths of the open sea.

Lances continue to puncture the flesh of the humpback, the first catch in many months, but the fight isn't over just yet, for the whale must be killed and then secured, secured from the lurches of the orca as they come in for the lips and tongue. The crews endeavour to impede the killers' efforts, try with all their might to drag the dead whale away, to be deblubbered at their convenience. This is but one of the many reasons that the killers soon decide to take their catch whilst near the mouth of the bay as opposed to within it, for the men of Twofold Bay seem to think that the whale is their just reward and should not be shared, and it was only due to the lack of a baleen plates, and little oil to quench the first of the market and merchants, that killers were not rendered into oil.

Twofold Bay was changing face, there was now Eden to the north of the bay and two other small villages, if that, upon the south, separated by the Kiah Inlet. There was Boyd Town to the west and East Boyd to the east.

1843

It had become more than clear, even to those that lived in denial over the growing absence of right whales, that bay whaling in Tasmania was coming to a close. But in lieu of the bay whalers of Twofold Bay the call to boats was made, quite often, with great regularity; not by time of day, but by the appearance of whales from June and on into the long winter months. The sighting of whales in and around Tasmanian bays might have taken a turn for the worst, but the slaughter in and around Twofold Bay had just commenced.

The tides were turning and the great phenomenon was taking shape. Boyd's empire collapsed completely, and the whaling gear no longer needed was sold to Alexander W. Davidson and his business partner Solomon Solomon, to sit idle for several years until the boats hit the water.

1849

Boyd departed Australia in 1849.

ORCINUS ORCA

1895

By 1895 sperm whaling was all but dead and the last unsuccessful hunt on the east coast concluded in 1896.

1955

The decline of humpback numbers, not due to the killers themselves, nor even the Davidson's, for the combined number of kills were rather deplorable to say the least; but particular investments such as those of the Norwegians, where whales were taken from Australian waters, certainly aided in the rise of situations within the world such as Frenchman Bay of West Australia taking the turn it did by commencing with sperm whaling and adding infuriation upon a depleted stock.

www.ingramcontent.com/pod-product-compliance
Lightning Source LLC
Chambersburg PA
CBHW020321010526
44107CB00054B/1927